Contents

Pension Trends

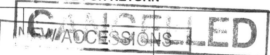

No. 1

2005 edition

Editors: Pauline Penneck

Di Lewis

Office for National Statistics

palgrave
macmillan

© Crown copyright 2005

Published with the permission of the Controller of Her Majesty's Stationery Office (HMSO).

This publication, excluding logos, may be reproduced free of charge, in any format or medium for research or private study subject to it being reproduced accurately and not used in a misleading context. The material must be acknowledged as Crown copyright and the title of the publication specified. This publication can also be accessed at the National Statistics website: **www.statistics.gov.uk**

For any other use of this material please apply for a free Click-Use Licence on the Office of Public Sector Information (OPSI) website:
www.opsi.gov.uk/click-use/index.htm

or write to The Licensing Division, St Clement's House,
2-16 Colegate, Norwich NR3 1BQ.
Fax 01603 723000 or email: hmsolicensing@cabinetoffice.x.gsi.gov.uk

First published 2005 by
PALGRAVE MACMILLAN
Houndmills, Basingstoke, Hampshire RG21 6XS and 175 Fifth Avenue, New York, NY 10010, USA
Companies and representatives throughout the world.

PALGRAVE MACMILLAN is the global academic imprint of the Palgrave Macmillan division of St. Martin's Press, LLC and of Palgrave Macmillan Ltd. Macmillan® is a registered trademark in the United States, United Kingdom and other countries. Palgrave is a registered trademark in the European Union and other countries.

ISBN 1-4039-9736-5

This book is printed on paper suitable for recycling and made from fully managed and sustained forest sources.

A catalogue record for this book is available from the British Library.

10 9 8 7 6 5 4 3 2 1
14 13 12 11 10 09 08 07 06 05

Printed and bound in Great Britain by Ashford Colour Press Ltd, Gosport.

A National Statistics publication

National Statistics are produced to high professional standards as set out in the National Statistics Code of Practice. They are produced free from political influence.

About the Office for National Statistics

The Office for National Statistics (ONS) is the government agency responsible for compiling, analysing and disseminating economic, social and demographic statistics about the United Kingdom. It also administers the statutory registration of births, marriages and deaths in England and Wales.

The Director of ONS is also the National Statistician and the Registrar General for England and Wales.

Contact points

For enquiries about this publication, contact the Editor
Email: pensionsanalysis@ons.gsi.gov.uk

For general enquiries, contact the National Statistics Customer Contact Centre.
Tel: **0845 601 3034** (minicom: 01633 812399)
Email: info@statistics.gsi.gov.uk
Fax: 01633 652747
Post: Room 1015, Government Buildings,
          Cardiff Road, Newport NP10 8XG

You can also find National Statistics on the Internet at:
www.statistics.gov.uk

List of figures and tables

5 Attitudes to retirement and pension planning

6 State pension entitlements and second tier pension provision

7 Private pension scheme membership

11 Employer pension provision

12 Pension fund investment

13 Pensions and the National Accounts

Preface

Scarcely a day goes by without a mention of pensions in the news. There are widespread concerns about the adequacy of people's income in retirement. These concerns are enhanced by the continuing increase in the length of time people survive to enjoy it.

At the same time pension statistics have found themselves under the most intense level of scrutiny. Figures have rightly been challenged by policy makers and commentators, and statisticians have begun to address shortcomings in underlying sources and methods. On the other hand the highly acclaimed report from the Pensions Commission is testament to the wealth of official information available to users.

As National Statistician I welcome the publication of *Pension Trends* as the first attempt by official statisticians to draw together all of these sources. The subject matter is very wide ranging, cutting across the whole range of official statistics from social through to economic, and looking at impacts from the perspective of individuals, companies and the country as a whole.

As with *Social Trends*, it will take time for *Pension Trends* to develop the best way of presenting these issues. But I consider it vital that the Office for National Statistics faces this challenge and seeks to provide an ongoing statistical backdrop to this important public debate.

Karen Dunnell
National Statistician
October 2005

Contributors

Authors:	Noor Ali
	Christina Forrest
	David Harper
	Di Lewis
	Pauline Penneck
	Geoff Tily
Editors:	Pauline Penneck
	Di Lewis

Acknowledgements

The Editors would like to thank all colleagues in contributing and reviewing government departments and other organisations including:

Department for Work and Pensions
Government Actuary's Department
The Institute for Fiscal Studies
Pensions Commission
Pensions Institute
HM Revenue and Customs
HM Treasury

Without their generous support and helpful comments this first edition of *Pension Trends* would not have been possible. Thanks also go to the following for their help in the production process:

Reviewers:	Jil Matheson
	Rich Wild
	Linda Zealey
Design and artwork:	Shain Bali
	Tony Castro
	Genevieve Chapman
	Andy Leach
	Desk Top Publications
Publishing management:	Paul Hyatt
	Phil Lewin

Symbols and conventions

Rounding of figures | In tables where figures have been rounded, there may be an apparent discrepancy between the sum of the constituent items and the total as shown.

Billion | This represents one thousand million.

Provisional and estimated data | Some data for the latest year (and occasionally for earlier years) are provisional or estimated. To minimise footnotes, these have not been indicated; source departments will be able to advise if revised data are available.

Financial years | 1 April 2003 to 31 March 2004, for example, is shown as 2003/04.

Combined years | Data covering more than one year, for example 2001, 2002 and 2003, is shown as 2001–03.

Units on tables | Figures representing percentages are shown in italics. Totals are shown in bold.

Symbols | The following symbols have been used in tables:
..   not available
.   not applicable
-    negligible (less than half the final digit shown)
0   nil

Introduction:
A framework for pension statistics

This is the first edition of *Pension Trends* – a new publication on pensions from the Office for National Statistics (ONS). *Pension Trends* brings together key statistics from a number of government departments and other organisations to illustrate the economic and social issues that shape trends in pension provision in the United Kingdom.

Many people have an interest in pensions and *Pension Trends* is aimed at a wide audience: policy makers in the public and private sectors; pension providers; journalists and other commentators; academics and students; and the general public – both current and future pensioners.

The range and complexity of factors that are relevant to pensions means that *Pension Trends* cannot attempt to cover everything on the subject in this first edition. Instead it highlights the core issues and provides pointers to the sources that provide more depth and detail. Relevant publications that may be of interest for further reading are also listed at the end of each chapter.

A framework for pension statistics

There is no single or concise way to encapsulate the complex issues regarding pensions that need to be illuminated by statistics and analysis. For example, there are a great number of factors that determine the retirement income of any particular cohort of individuals at any point in time. Bringing them together in a clear and coherent way is not straightforward.

'Frameworks' help provide a structure to present and understand statistics on complex issues. In economic statistics, for example, there is a long established and highly developed framework – the National Accounts. Two examples in other areas are the frameworks that have been developed by ONS for health statistics and for labour market statistics.[1]

Any framework for pension statistics is perhaps more wide-ranging, as factors influencing pension provision and pension income cut across both the economic and social domains of statistics and policy. Moreover analysis needs to examine these factors at various levels, looking at individual and household activities and circumstances, as well as those of businesses, and national and international perspectives.

Pension provision and incomes also change over time and between cohorts. The time dimension extends over a long scale; the pension for any particular individual will be influenced by factors prevalent at their birth and during their upbringing, such as health and education. These in turn have an impact on their working-age life and ability to build up resources on which they can draw throughout their retirement. The 'cohort' dimension recognises the difference in circumstances for specific groups of people – those born in the 1990s as distinct from those born in the 1930s, for example.

Pension Trends broadly follows the general format of this framework, examining the interaction of social and economic issues across households, corporations and

Contact

The Editor

Pensions Analysis Unit
Office for National Statistics
Government Buildings
Cardiff Road
Newport
Gwent NP10 8XG

Email: pensionsanalysis@ons.gov.uk

government, looking at trends through time and across cohorts where possible. The first two chapters set out the wider social context for pension policy, looking first at the main legislative changes on pensions over the last century to provide a context for understanding the mix of arrangements that are in place. The second chapter sets out the demographic context looking back over the same period and forward into the next 50 years.

Chapter 3 might be viewed from either the individual or wider economic context. It examines labour market conditions over the period for which data are available; the discussion looks at general labour market trends, in particular male/female employment changes, and then at specific labour market trends for older workers.

The individual perspective is the focus of chapters 4 to 10. These cover both current pensioners and future pensioners and cut across various economic and social aspects of pensions as they affect individuals. In turn they discuss actual incomes received in retirement; expectations of retirement; the use of state provision and private provision; contributions to various schemes; and the ways that future pensioners are building pension entitlements or planning to increase retirement incomes by other means, by looking at stocks of both pension wealth and other sources of household wealth, for example in housing or equities.

Chapters 11 and 12 move on to the corporate sector. Chapter 11 examines pensions from the perspective of the provider – businesses and pension schemes – while chapter 12 discusses issues from the perspective of the financial sector, in particular addressing the investment behaviour of pension funds.

Finally chapter 13 takes the discussion to the national level, analysing state and private pensions in the context of the National Accounts, looking at the household, corporate and government sectors.

Users of these pension statistics need to recognise the issues of risk and uncertainty. Any measurements, be they of past trends, the current position or future changes, are subject to error. This is particularly the case for pensions given the complexity of the provision at any one time and the long timescales – both looking back and projecting forward – which are relevant to pension issues. For instance, actual population in the future is unlikely to exactly match the projections and users should take on board the associated uncertainty. It is quite likely that in the future, users, policy makers and data providers will all be looking to a fuller quantification of these uncertainties, but the limitations of statistics should be recognised when bringing them to bear on analysis of pension issues.

Future editions of *Pension Trends* will incorporate analyses from new data sources that may become available and will aim to reflect developing thinking about the framework for pension statistics. Some may give more emphasis to factors and institutional impacts that have received less attention here. As this is a new publication, the editorial team would welcome readers' views on *Pension Trends*. Please write to or email the Editor at the contact address provided on the previous page.

Definitions and terms

A list of symbols and conventions used in this publication can be found on page xiii. Non-specialist readers may find the Glossary at the end of the publication useful.

Availability on electronic media

Pension Trends is available electronically as an interactive PDF via the National Statistics website, www.statistics.gov.uk/ pensiontrends. This PDF contains links to Excel spreadsheets giving data for all tables and figures.

References

1   The framework for health statistics was first set out in *Health Inequalities* (ONS, 1997). The framework for labour market statistics is set out in the *National Statistics Quarterly Review* Series Report No. 11: Review of the Framework for Labour Market Statistics, 2002, www.statistics.gov.uk/methods_quality/ quality_review/labour.asp#nsqr

Pensions legislation: an overview

Chapter 1

Figure 1.1

Pensions legislation timeline, 1900 to 2004

1900

1908 *Old Age Pensions Act*
Non-contributory means tested state pensions for the over-70s

1911 *National Insurance Act*
Compulsory NI contributions to insure against sickness/unemployment

1921 *Finance Act*
Tax relief for contributions to occupational pension schemes

1925 *Widows, Orphans and Old Age Contributory Pensions Act*
Contributory pensions for 65 to 70 year olds and maintenance for widows

1940 *Old Age and Widows Pensions Act*
Means tested benefits extended to pensioners and their widows. Women's pension age lowered to 60

1946 *National Insurance Act*
Universal social insurance system – flat-rate benefits from flat-rate NI contributions

1947 *Finance Act*
Limits on level of tax relief for occupational pension contributions

1948 *National Assistance Act*
Extended and consolidated means-tested safety net

1959 *National Insurance Act*
Introduced state graduated retirement benefit scheme

1973 *Social Security Act*
Contributions fully earnings-related. State graduated retirement benefit scheme wound up
Regulation of occupational schemes

1974 *National Insurance Act*
State pensions to be uprated by the better of prices or earnings

1975 *Social Security Pensions Act*
Introduced state earnings-related pension scheme (SERPS)

1980 *Social Security Act*
State pension uprating to be based on price only

1986 *Social Security Act*
Cutbacks in SERPS; wider options for private pensions

1995 *Pensions Act*
Equalisation of state pension age for men and women phased in from 2010. Stronger regulatory framework

1999 *Welfare Reform and Pensions Act*
Introduced stakeholder pensions

2000 *Child Support, Pensions and Social Security Act*
Replaced SERPS with state second pension

2002 *Pension Credit Act*
Guaranteed minimum income with tapered benefit for all over-60s

2004 *Finance Act*
Simplified tax regime for pensions

2004 *Pensions Act*
Reformed pensions regulatory system

This chapter provides an overview of the main legislative changes over the last century, which reflect the thinking of successive governments on provision for old age. It provides a context for understanding the mix of arrangements in place that are described in subsequent chapters.

Laying the foundations

At the beginning of the 20th century the only general support for old age was through the Poor Law. Only a small minority of white-collar and public service workers had access to pensions from employment. Though many workers had some mutual insurance, the Friendly Societies did not cover old age.

Following pioneering surveys showing the extent of poverty among the elderly, there was intense debate over how to provide better support. This finally resulted in Lloyd George's *Old Age Pensions Act 1908*. From January 1909, a non-contributory pension of 5 shillings (25 pence) a week became payable to each person over 70 with an income less than 8 shillings a week. Reduced amounts were paid to those with incomes up to 12 shillings a week.

The Liberal Government went on to introduce contributory insurance against sickness and unemployment in the *National Insurance Act 1911*. In 1925 the contributory principle was extended to pensions by the *Widows, Orphans and Old Age Contributory Pensions Act*. Coming into effect in 1928, the Act provided maintenance outside the Poor Law for widows and grafted contributory pensions from age 65 over the existing non-contributory scheme. Pensions required contributions in the five years before 65; those without a recent contribution record were still subject to a means test at age 70. Like other insurance benefits under the 1911 Act, National Insurance pension coverage was not universal and was aimed mainly at lower paid and manual workers. It did not provide support for dependants. However, a married woman could use her husband's contribution record to gain a pension when she reached 65.

During this period occupational pensions grew steadily. The *Finance Act 1921* introduced tax relief on pension scheme contributions and investments, placing them on the same footing as savings through Friendly Societies and life insurance. The *Finance Act 1947* introduced limits on the amount of tax relief allowable on pensions.

The welfare state

By the outbreak of the Second World War, the foundations had been laid for a basic flat-rate state pension entitlement, but the system was by no means comprehensive. The flat rate benefit of 10 shillings (50 pence) was not enough by itself to meet subsistence needs, but no additional help was available except through the Poor Law. Benefits had not been increased since 1919.

In 1935, a new national means-tested assistance scheme had been introduced for the unemployed. This was intended to meet full subsistence needs, including housing costs. The *Old Age and Widows Pensions Act 1940* of the war-time National Government now extended this supplementary assistance to pensioners and widows, removing them from the scope of the Poor Law. In addition the Act reduced women's pension age to 60.

In 1942, William Beveridge's report *Social Insurance and Allied Services* mapped the way to the creation of the post-war 'cradle to grave' welfare state. The new Labour Government's *National Insurance Act 1946* created a universal social insurance system based around flat-rate benefits (at the same level for all contingencies) in return for flat-rate contributions. Entitlement to pension was based on earnings across the whole working life, and for the first time became dependent on retirement from work, as well as age. Married women were encouraged not to insure personally. Instead, they could obtain a retirement pension of 60 per cent of their husband's entitlement.

The new universal National Insurance system was backed up by a comprehensive safety net – National Assistance. In effect, the *National Assistance Act 1948* extended to all groups the means-tested benefits previously available to the elderly and the unemployed. Beveridge wanted insurance benefits to be set at subsistence level, so that recourse to National Assistance would be the exception for those with extra needs. However, the National Government had taken the view – shared by successive administrations – that it was not feasible to pay flat-rate benefits at a rate high enough to cope with variations in individual need, the most important of which was rent.

Though post-war benefits were much higher than their predecessors, the means-tested safety net continued to play a significant role in the support system for old age. By the end of 1950, people over state pension age constituted nearly two thirds of the National Assistance caseload. There were several attempts during the 1950s to reduce reliance on means-tested benefits in old age by increasing National Insurance pension rates. But it was increasingly clear that flat-rate benefits, at a level supportable by flat-rate National Insurance contributions, could not achieve this objective. Political thinkers began to see the development of a second, earnings-linked pension as the key to resolving poverty in retirement.

Towards a second pension

For the next 20 years, the parties competed to produce plans for 'national superannuation' – to give all old people the additional resources enjoyed by those with occupational pensions. The first to see the statute book, in the *National Insurance Act 1959*, was the state graduated retirement benefit scheme, which came into effect in 1961. This introduced important new concepts to UK social security. For the first time National Insurance contributions became partly earnings-related and extra contributions bought units of additional pension on top of the basic. An element of risk relation was introduced – women paid more per unit than men to reflect their greater longevity. And employers with occupational pension schemes were allowed to 'contract out' (see Glossary) of the additional contributions.

The graduated retirement benefit scheme served an immediate purpose in assuring the solvency of the National Insurance Fund, but it was quickly clear that it would not create a sufficient second pension. As inflation began to rise in the late 1960s, protecting the lifetime value of all types of pensions and pension savings also became an issue.

Between 1969 and 1975 there were various attempts to legislate for a more wide-ranging reform of pensions, though reflecting very different views of the way forward. The new Conservative administration of 1970 took the view that second pensions should generally be provided through the expansion and improvement of occupational schemes. The *Social Security Act 1973* therefore proposed a limited direct role for the state in running a modest 'reserve' scheme – with an invested fund element – for people who did not have access to occupational pensions. But it also established powers to regulate occupational schemes – through a new Occupational Pensions Board – and to drive up their standards, for example by requiring the protection of early leavers. National Insurance contributions were to be fully earnings-related, and the graduated retirement benefit scheme wound up.

Following the February 1974 election, the new Labour government did not proceed with the state reserve scheme although it preserved the other elements of the package. Its White Paper *Better Pensions*, published in September 1974, set out a more ambitious role for the state, aimed in particular at improving the position of women and lower earners. The proposals – enacted as the *Social Security Pensions Act 1975* and implemented from April 1978 – envisaged a reformed state pension scheme built around two elements: a basic pension and an additional earnings-related pension accruing at 25 per cent of relevant earnings.

Rights to the new additional pension, the value of which would be protected in line with earnings as they accrued, would build up over a maximum of 20 years and then would be based on the best 20 years' earnings. Men and women would earn equal pension for equal contributions: married women would no longer be able to opt out, though non-working years looking after children would be excluded from the calculation. There would be better rights for survivors.

The new state earnings-related pension scheme (SERPS) was seen as providing a benchmark for occupational pensions. Occupational pension schemes that guaranteed at least equivalent benefits could contract out of SERPS, paying a lower rate of National Insurance contribution. Schemes took responsibility for paying the guaranteed minimum pension, but the state assumed responsibility for price-protecting its value once in payment.

Protecting the value of pensions in payment

Until 1971, state retirement pensions and other benefits had not been increased annually. Rising inflation made protecting the value of pensions a contentious issue throughout the decade. From 1973, statutory annual upratings were introduced, and on the change of government, the *National Insurance Act 1974* provided that retirement pensions and other long-term benefits should be increased by the better of prices or earnings. However after a further change of administration the *Social Security Act 1980* reverted to protection by prices only.

Revisiting the role of the state

During the 1980s, concerns about the long-term cost of better state pensions led – in the *Social Security Act 1986* – to cutbacks in SERPS, coupled with efforts to encourage a more varied and flexible non-state pensions sector. There was particular concern that existing occupational pensions disadvantaged 'early leavers' – workers who changed jobs frequently, leaving many small pension funds.

With effect from the end of the century, the 1986 Act abolished the best 20 years provision in SERPS, reduced the accrual rate from 25 per cent to 20 per cent and halved survivors' rights. From 1988, it introduced a new form of personal money purchase pension scheme. Employers could no longer make membership of their occupational pension scheme compulsory, while workers could opt out of both SERPS and occupational pension schemes on an individual basis, using National Insurance contribution rebates to fund a portable personal pension. The new schemes were initially made more attractive by an extra 'incentive' rebate. In addition, employers now also took limited responsibility for the price-protection of pensions in payment.

The changes aimed to broaden options for private pension saving and assist mobile workers. However, the contribution rebate alone was inadequate to fund a personal pension without additional employer or employee contributions. Often these were not made. Some workers also made inappropriate choices, sometimes on the basis of poor advice. More generally, the changes encouraged a trend towards 'defined contribution' rather than 'defined benefit' schemes (see Glossary), leaving the risk of investment fluctuations to be borne more heavily by the future pensioner.

At the same time, new EU directives and judgments directed at securing equal treatment for men and women began to affect UK pensions. In the *Pensions Act 1995,* the Government took steps to equalise pension age at 65, to be phased in between 2010 and 2020. It also strengthened the regulatory framework for non-state pensions, following the Maxwell scandal in which pension funds were misappropriated by the employer.

Recent pension reform

The stated policy of the Government elected in 1997 has been to seek to improve the position of existing pensioners. A substantial proportion of pensioners continued to be reliant on means-tested benefits, but many who were eligible did not claim them and there was long-standing resentment that the safety-net appeared not to reward thrift. Income support for pensioners was firstly restructured as the Minimum Income Guarantee and secondly – through the *Pension Credit Act 2002* – replaced with a different scheme. Pension Credit, introduced in October 2003, guarantees a minimum income to all over-60s; above the minimum, benefit is tapered away where there are savings, rather than being withdrawn £1 for £1. The Government also committed itself to increasing Pension Credit in line with earnings for a period.

The *Welfare Reform and Pensions Act 1999* sought to make private pensions more accessible and secure to lower earners by legislating for 'stakeholder pensions' that met tests of quality and cost. These were introduced in 2001. The *Child Support, Pensions and Social Security Act 2000* created an improved state second pension (S2P) from 2002 for those on lower earnings.

Since the beginning of the 21st century there has been rising concern about the adequacy of the pension system in the face of demographic change (see chapter 2), together with high-profile insolvencies and a number of closures of defined benefit schemes. This led to intensive debate about how best to stimulate pension saving, balance the interests of workers, pensioners, employers, government and the pensions industry, and secure the long-term future. A series of reports and

enquiries led up the Green Paper *Simplicity, Security and Choice: Working and Saving for Retirement* in 2002.

This proposed a simplification of the tax regime for pensions, replacing the eight existing tax regimes with a single universal regime. Enacted in the *Finance Act 2004,* the changes come into effect in 2006. The *Pensions Act 2004* reformed the pensions regulatory system, setting up a new Pensions Regulator, and among other changes introduced new levy-based schemes to protect the interests of members whose final salary schemes fail.

Alongside this, an independent Pensions Commission was established to take stock of the whole pensions picture: its final report, with policy recommendations, is expected in late 2005.

Sources and further reading

Blake, D (2003) *Pension Schemes and Pension Funds in the United Kingdom,* Oxford University Press.

Department for Work and Pensions (2002) *Simplicity, Security and Choice: Working and Saving for Retirement,* Green Paper, Cm 5677. The Stationery Office.

Department for Work and Pensions, (2004) *Simplicity, Security and Choice: Informed Choices for Working and Saving,* February 2004, Cm 6111. The Stationery Office.

Gilbert, B, (1966) *The Evolution of National Insurance in Great Britain,* Michael Joseph, London.

Pensions Commission (2004) *Pensions: Challenges and Choices,* the first report of the Pensions Commission. The Stationery Office. The second report is due to be published late November 2005.

Population change

- In 2003 there were 3.3 people of working age for each person of pensionable age in the United Kingdom. This figure is expected to fall to 2.3 by 2051.

- There were greater numbers of people aged between 35 and 39 than in any other age band. By 2051 it is projected that the greatest number of people will be in the 60 to 64 age band.

- The old age dependency ratio increased from around 20 per cent in the 1960s to around 27 per cent between 1980 and 2003, and is projected to rise to around 47 per cent by 2051.

- Men aged 65 in 1981 could expect on average to live a further 14 years and women a further 18 years. By 2051, men aged 65 could expect to live a further 22 years and women a further 24.

- Migration is currently acting against the ageing of the population. The inflow of migrants to the United Kingdom exceeded the outflow by just over 1 million people over the whole period between 1993 and 2002.

- Projections are for a continuing net inflow consisting mostly of individuals of working age. This would produce lower old age dependency ratios, but the long-term effect would be limited if migrants settle and age in this country.

The ageing population

Over the 20th century the UK population aged. Life expectancy rose while fertility rates broadly declined (with the exception of the immediate periods following both world wars, and the 1960s) and older people accounted for a proportionately larger share of the population over time. Apart from a very slight rise in fertility in 2003, these changes have continued into the start of the 21st century and, according to official population projections, are expected to continue for at least the next 50 years.

In the United Kingdom in 2003 there were 3.3 people of working age (16 to state pension age, see Glossary) for each person of pensionable age. This compared with 3.6 in 1971, and is projected to be 2.3 in 2051 (even allowing for the increase in state pension age to 65 for women that will be phased in between 2010 and 2020).[1]

While longer life expectancy is a favourable trend, the ageing population has implications for a number of policy areas such as health and care, and is of particular importance for pension policy. Other things being equal, pensions will have to be paid to more people for longer periods of time.

The demographic changes have a similar impact on all types of pension provision, whether state pensions funded by taxation or private pensions funded by assets, the value of which is underpinned by economic activity. Such changes are common to nearly all developed countries.

The age structure of a population is often presented as a 'population pyramid' that shows the proportions of the population in different age bands by sex. Figure 2.1 shows the population pyramid for 2003 and for the projected age structure of the population in 2051. The bulk of the distribution is seen to be moving up the age axis – the 2003 'bulge' between ages 30 and 45 is less marked and there are greater numbers of people aged 55 and over in 2051. From this perspective, the ageing population has been characterised as a change from a population pyramid to a population column.

Dependency ratios can indicate changes to the structure of the population over time. The most common, and most helpful for pensions analysis, is the old age dependency ratio, which gives the number of people above pensionable age as a proportion of the number of people of working age. A ratio based on a specific age does not reflect any changes in economic activity among those over pensionable age – this is discussed in chapter 3.

Figure **2.1**

Current and projected distribution of the UK population: by sex and age, 2003 and 2051
United Kingdom

Millions

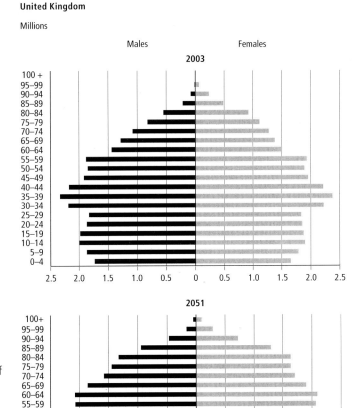

Source: 2003-based principal population projections, Government Actuary's Department

The following analysis uses the age definition 20 to 64 for working age and 65 and over for pensionable age. This is to provide a consistent analysis through time given the change in state pension age for women and the fact that increasingly people are remaining in education beyond the age of 16. Figure 2.2 shows the old age dependency ratio increasing steadily from around 20 per cent in the 1960s and levelling off at around 27 per cent between 1980 and 2003. The ratio is projected to remain around this level until 2010. Increases are then projected to resume as the large cohorts born after the Second World War reach age 65, with the ratio reaching an estimated 47 per cent in 2051.

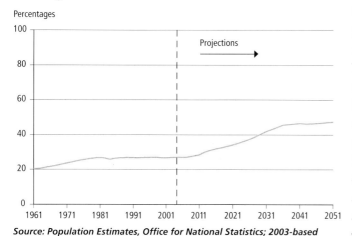

Figure **2.2**

Old age dependency ratio

United Kingdom

Percentages

Source: Population Estimates, Office for National Statistics; 2003-based
principal population projections, Government Actuary's Department

There are three main determinants that drive population
change and hence trends in the old age dependency ratio:
fertility, mortality and migration.

Figure 2.3 illustrates trends in fertility and mortality using birth
and death rates, which express the number of births and
deaths in a specific period relative to the size of the population.

Mortality

Over the whole of the 20th century the crude death rate (see
Glossary) fell from 16 per 1,000 to 10 per 1,000. This decrease
has occurred despite the population increasing and having a
growing share of older people. Improvements in mortality
rates have meant that people on average are living longer.
These improvements have affected the age distribution in two
distinct phases. In the first half of the 20th century, advances
in the prevention of infectious and respiratory diseases led to
a great reduction in infant and child mortality. In the latter
part of the century, the most dramatic mortality
improvements were due to a reduction in death from
circulatory diseases (in part caused by the decline in smoking)
and these affected mainly older people. In terms of the old
age dependency ratio, survival rates both up to age 65 (the
working age population) and after (the retired population) are
important. The 20th century saw a strong steady increase in
the proportion of the population surviving up to age 65 and,
in the latter part of the century, rises in the proportions
surviving from age 65 to older ages. These changes to
mortality alone would have led to an ageing population
throughout the 20th and into the 21st century.

Improvements in life expectancy at age 65 are projected to
continue into the future (Figure 2.4). In 1981, male life
expectancy at age 65 was 14 years; this is projected to have

Figure **2.3**

Crude birth and death rates[1]

England & Wales

Rates per 1,000 population

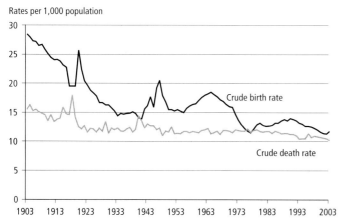

1 See Glossary for an explanation of crude birth and death rates.

Source: Office for National Statistics

Figure **2.4**

Historic and projected cohort life expectancy[1] at 65

United Kingdom

Years

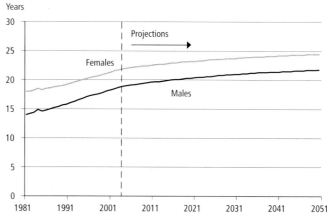

1 See Glossary for a definition of cohort life expectancy.

**Source: Population Estimates, Office for National Statistics; 2003-based
principal population projections, Government Actuary's Department**

9

increased to 19 years by 2005 and to 22 years by 2051. The corresponding projections for females are from 18 years, increasing to 22 years in 2005 and 24 years by 2051.

Figure 2.4 also illustrates the longstanding differences in life expectancy between men and women. Based on the latest projections, women aged 65 in 2003 could expect to live on average three years longer than men. The cause of this difference is still a matter of some debate – for example, it might reflect differences in attitudes to health and healthy activities, changes in labour market participation over time, or genetic factors. A modest degree of convergence in male and female life expectancy is anticipated to continue.

Fertility

As Figure 2.2 indicates, in spite of a continuous improvement in mortality, the old age dependency ratio has been flat since the end of the 20th century. This reflects the sizes of cohorts that were largely determined by the fertility trends illustrated in Figure 2.3: the relatively low fertility in the 1920s and 1930s, the sharp increases in fertility just after the First and Second World Wars and during the 1960s, and the subsequent fall in fertility to the below replacement levels that have prevailed since the early 1970s. The levelling out of the old age dependency ratio from the 1970s followed as those born during these 'baby booms' entered the workforce with a cumulative effect. The rise in the old age dependency ratio, forecast to begin around 2010, follows as these individuals reach retirement age against a backdrop of ongoing low fertility that is projected to continue for the next 50 years.

Many reasons have been put forward for the changes in fertility behaviour over the last century. The most common explanation for the baby boom of the 1960s is as a consequence of the optimism and prosperity of the post-war era, coupled with changes in social attitudes, leading to earlier childbearing. Conversely the lower fertility over the past 30 years is widely regarded as reflecting the increased choices in education and employment, delayed childbearing, and further changes in social attitudes. Widespread availability of effective birth control also allows more choices about timing and spacing of births, as well as overall family size.

Migration

The aspect of demographic change that is currently acting against the ageing of the population is migration. Over the past decade migration into the United Kingdom has been the most substantial component of population change and, in turn, affects future projections of population and dependency ratios.

The change in the total population depends on natural change (the difference between numbers of births and deaths), and migration. Figure 2.5 shows the respective contributions, with net migration measured as the difference between the inflow to, and outflow from, the United Kingdom.

Between 1971 and the early 1990s nearly all of the increase in population was due to natural change. Over the first half of the 1990s the increase in natural change began to diminish and net migration began to rise. Then between 1997 and 1999 there was a sharp increase, and net migration has remained at a relatively high level ever since. Looking at figures for net migration over ten year periods: between 1973 and 1982 there was a net outflow of 430,000 people; between 1983 and 1992 a net inflow of 240,000 people; and between 1993 and 2002 a net inflow of just over 1 million.[2]

Figure 2.5

Annual population change[1]

United Kingdom

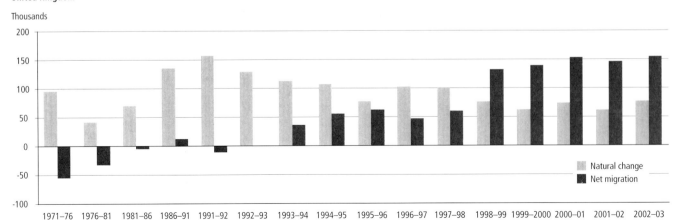

1 Change from mid-year to mid-year population estimates. Between 1971 and 1991 changes are annual averages of five-year periods.

Source: Population Trends, Office for National Statistics

The Government Actuary's Department projections based on in 2003 assume a net inflow of 130,000 people each year throughout the projection period. As with past migration this net inflow is assumed to consist mostly of individuals of working age. A higher level of future net migration would produce lower old age dependency ratios, but the long-term effect would be limited if migrants settle and age in this country.

Uncertainty

All projected trends have a degree of uncertainty that increases the further into the future that projections are made. Back in 1993, the Office of Population, Censuses and Surveys (which later joined with the Central Statistical Office to form the Office for National Statistics) observed that 'Indeed the one certainty of making projections is that, due to the inherent uncertainty of demographic behaviour, they will turn out to be wrong as a forecast of future demographic events or population structure'.[3] As part of the process of making projections plausible, alternative scenarios (variants) are produced looking at variation in each of the three main demographic components, both individually and combined. Population projections and variants can be found on the Government Actuary's Department website.

Nevertheless, the rise in the old age dependency ratio that is at the centre of the pension policy debate has been caused by historic trends. It may be that future fertility will turn out to be higher than predicted and life expectancy lower, but the differences would have to be very substantial to affect significantly the rise in the old age dependency ratio by the middle of the century. On the other hand it may be that fertility will be lower, mortality improvements will be greater and migration will be lower than anticipated, and the rise in the old age dependency ratio will be even more marked. Demographers regularly review assumptions to take account of the latest statistics on births, deaths and migration, and the official projections, including the variants, remain the most authoritative guide to demographic change in the future.

References

1. This chapter uses 2003-based population projections; these have now been superseded with the release of 2004-based projections. Processing considerations and publication scheduling meant that it was not possible to use these later figures.

2. Office for National Statistics (2004) *Focus on People and Migration*. ONS: London.

3. Office of Population, Censuses and Surveys (1993) *1991-based national population projections*, PP2 no. 18, p.27. HMSO: London.

Sources and further reading

The Government Actuary's Department website gives population projections and variants.
www.gad.gov.uk

Office for National Statistics (2004) *Focus on People and Migration*. ONS: London web publication, www.statistics.gov.uk/focuson/migration/

Office for National Statistics. Gjonça A, Tomassini C, Toson B and Smallwood S (2005) 'Sex differences in mortality, a comparison of the United Kingdom and other developed countries', *Health Statistics Quarterly*, No. 26 Summer 2005. www.statistics.gov.uk/downloads/theme_health/HSQ26.pdf

Office for National Statistics *Population Trends*. Palgrave Macmillan: Basingstoke. In particular, Shaw C (2004) 'Interim 2003-based national population projections for the United Kingdom and constituent countries' *Population Trends*, No. 118 Winter 2004 and Smallwood S and Chamberlain J (2005) 'Replacement fertility, what has it been and what does it mean?', *Population Trends*, No. 119 Spring 2005.

Pensions Commission (2004) *Pensions: Challenges and Choices; The First Report of the Pensions Commission*. The Stationery Office: London.

The labour market and retirement

- In 1971 the male employment rate was 91.2 per cent; in 2004 it was 79.3 per cent. Over the same period the female employment rate rose from 58.0 per cent to 69.6 per cent.

- The employment rate for both men and women declines steadily from around age 50 onwards and at age 64 fewer than half of men are in work (spring 2005).

- Employment rates rose between 2000 and 2004 for both men and women in the age groups 50 to state pension age, and over state pension age, reaching the highest level in published time series that begin in 1984.

- In spring 2005 the employment rate for men of state pension age and over was 8.9 per cent while for women it was 10.4 per cent.

- 11 per cent of women considered themselves retired in the five years before their state pension age compared with 33 per cent of men in the five years before their state pension age.

- 63 per cent of those with private pension income retired before state pension age compared with 55 per cent of those without a private pension income.

This chapter examines trends in labour market participation and the transition towards retirement. The old age dependency ratio described in chapter 2 shows the number of people above pensionable age as a proportion of the number of people of working age. In the context of pensions, it is also important to examine the share of each age group that is working. Over the past 35 years there have been substantial changes in these shares as well as in the composition of the labour market. This discussion examines trends in economic activity and participation by age and sex, with a particular focus on the labour force participation of older age groups on either side of the state pension age (SPA, see Glossary).

Employment and unemployment

Unemployment has been falling over the last ten years, with the number of unemployed people (according to the ILO definition, see box) falling from 3.0 million in 1993 to 1.4 million in 2004. Figure 3.1 illustrates how both the employment and unemployment rates have returned to levels last experienced at the start of the 1970s. In 2004, the unemployment rate was 4.9 per cent – the lowest annual figure since 1975. Equally, employment rates are relatively high. In 2004, the employment rate was 74.7 per cent, the second highest figure since 1975 (it was 75.0 per cent in 1990).

Figure **3.1**

Employment and unemployment rates
United Kingdom

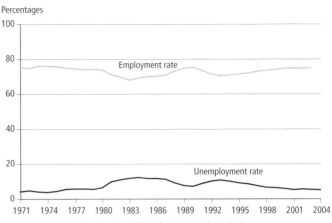

Source: Labour Force Survey, Office for National Statistics

However, this aggregate story masks important trends in the rates of employment by age and sex. Table 3.2 presents key labour market rates for men and women between 1971 and 2004.

Definitions of employment status

Employment

People who are in employment may be employees, self-employed or on a government-supported training programme. The International Labour Organisation's (ILO's) definition of the employment rate is the percentage of people in a given age group who are in one or more hours of paid employment a week. Employment rates can be presented for any population group and are the proportion of that group who are in employment. Rates used in this chapter are based on employment as a share of the working-age population, defined as age 16 to state pension age.

Unemployment

The ILO's definition of unemployment is people who are without a job, who want a job, have actively sought work in the last four weeks and are available to start work in the next two weeks; or people who are out of work and have found a job and are waiting to start it in the next two weeks. Rates used in this chapter are based on unemployment as a share of the working-age population, defined as age 16 to state pension age.

Economic activity

The labour market can be divided into two groups: the economically active and inactive. The economically active are defined as those who are either in employment or who are unemployed and actively seeking work.

Economic inactivity

Economic inactivity refers to people who are neither in employment nor unemployed, and who are not actively seeking work, for example, people who have retired or are long term sick. The Labour Force Survey categorises all economically inactive people who are more than five years above the state pension age as retired. The economic inactivity rate for an age group is the number of people who are inactive as a percentage of the total population of that age. Rates used in this chapter are based on the working-age population, defined as age 16 to state pension age.

Table **3.2**

The labour market, 1971 to 2004[1]

United Kingdom
Percentages

	Employment	Unemployment	Inactivity
All			
1971–75	75.3	4.0	21.6
1976–80	74.1	5.7	21.5
1981–85	69.4	11.1	21.9
1986–90	72.6	9.2	20.1
1991–95	71.3	9.6	21.1
1996–2000	73.2	6.8	21.5
2001–04	74.6	5.1	21.4
Change over period	-0.7	1.1	-0.2
Males			
1971–75	91.2	3.4	5.6
1976–80	87.6	5.2	7.6
1981–85	79.2	11.5	10.5
1986–90	80.3	9.4	11.5
1991–95	76.6	11.1	13.8
1996–2000	78.1	7.6	15.4
2001–04	79.3	5.5	16.1
Change over period	-11.9	2.1	10.5
Females			
1971–75	58.0	5.1	38.9
1976–80	59.4	6.3	36.5
1981–85	58.8	10.5	34.3
1986–90	64.3	8.9	29.4
1991–95	65.6	7.7	28.9
1996–2000	67.9	5.8	27.9
2001–04	69.6	4.6	27.0
Change over period	11.6	-0.5	-11.9

1 Averaged over five-year periods except for 2001–04, which is averaged
over a four-year period.

Source: Labour Force Survey, Office for National Statistics

Over this period the employment rate of 74.6 per cent for 2001–04 was only marginally lower than the rate of 75.3 per cent for 1971–75. However, the employment rate by sex shows a more significant change. Over the same period:

- the male employment rate has fallen by 11.9 percentage points, from 91.2 per cent to 79.3 per cent; and

- the female employment rate has risen by 11.6 percentage points, from 58.0 per cent to 69.6 per cent.

Figure 3.3 shows annual figures for the employment rate by sex. It shows the main fall in the male employment rate was between 1972 and 1983, with a particularly abrupt fall during the 1980–81 recession; there was a degree of recovery in the second half of the 1980s, but this reversed in the 1991 recession and recent improvements have only just gone beyond the 1983 position. The female employment rate did not change greatly until 1983 when it began to increase rapidly; it fell back less far than the male employment rate in the 1991 recession and then increased steadily over the rest of the 1990s and 2000s to reach a peak of 70.1 per cent in 2005. Part-time employment is more important for women than for men although shares for men have been increasing; in spring 2005, 10.7 per cent of men and 47.8 per cent of women were in part-time employment. In 1971 the gap between the overall male and female employment rates was 35.5 per cent; in 2005 it was 9.1 per cent.

Figure **3.3**

Employment rates:[1] by sex

United Kingdom

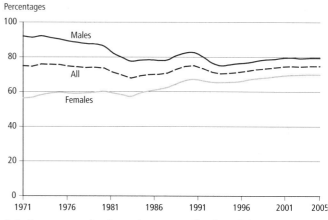

1 Spring quarters of each year from seasonally adjusted data. Males aged
16 to 64, females aged 16 to 59. The percentage of the population that
is in employment.

Source: Labour Force Survey, Office for National Statistics

Over the full period of the comparison, the change in male employment has not resulted in an increase in unemployment. Instead there has been an increase in the number of men classified as economically inactive (see box). Between 1971–75 and 2000–04, despite a drop in the male employment rate by 11.9 per cent, the male unemployment rate only increased by 2.1 per cent while inactivity for men increased by 10.5 per cent.

This change is widely understood as following from the decline in the manufacturing industry over the same period. Manufacturing activity fell sharply through the 1974–75 and 1980–81 recessions. Between 1973 and 1982 the official index of manufacturing output fell by 18 per cent.

Manufacturing employment fell alongside output. Official statistics for employment by sector only begin in 1978, but show a decline of manufacturing employment from 7.1 million in 1978 to 5.5 million in 1983. Full data are not available, but the evidence suggests that job losses were disproportionately concentrated among older age groups. The older workers who lost their jobs had more difficulty finding new work and many ended up, more or less permanently, on invalidity/incapacity benefits and were therefore likely not to be recorded as unemployed. Research published in 1992 by David Coleman, Professor of Demography at Oxford and John Salt, Professor of Geography at University College London showed male economic activity between 1961 and 1981 only slightly changed for all age groups under age 44, but larger changes for all older age groups. Over the period 1961 to 1981, they record a fall in the male employment rate from 91.2 per cent to 72.0 per cent in the group aged 55 to 65 and a fall from 24.4 to 10.3 per cent in the group aged 65 and over.

The age structure of employment and changes over time

For both men and women, the employment rate is highest in the 25 to 34 and 35 to 49 age groups and then begins to fall (Figure 3.4). Taking the most recent period for which data are available, spring 2005, the male employment rate was 86.6 per cent for those aged 35 to 49, compared with 72.3 per cent for those aged 50 to SPA. Similarly, for women the employment rate was 76.1 per cent for those aged 35 to 49, compared with 67.7 per cent for those aged 50 to 60. In practice analyses of figures by individual year age groups show the employment rate for both men and women fell steadily from around age 50 onwards, and at age 64 fewer than half of men are in work. These patterns within the broad age groups are examined in more detail in a later section on retirement.

Employment rates for women and men seemingly diverge alongside child rearing. In both the oldest and youngest age groups the female employment rate is higher than the male employment rate. In 2005, for 16 to 17 year olds the male employment rate was 38.7 per cent and the female employment rate 42.5 per cent; for those of SPA and over, the male employment rate was 8.9 per cent and the female employment rate 10.4 per cent (although the latter comparison is not consistent because the female group starts at 60 and the male at 65). For all other age groups the employment rates for women were lower than for men. The largest difference was in the main age group for child rearing: for those aged 25 to 34 the employment rate for men of 87.7 per cent was 14.8 percentage points higher than the rate for women.

Figure 3.4

Employment rates:[1] by sex and age,[2] spring 2005

United Kingdom

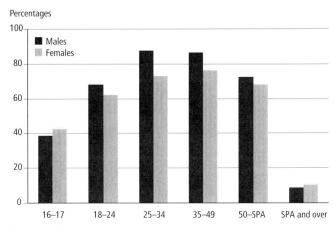

Percentages

1 Seasonally adjusted.
2 State pension age (SPA) is currently 60 for women and 65 for men.

Source: Labour Force Survey, Office for National Statistics

Table 3.5 shows how the age structure of the labour market has changed over nearly the whole period for which official figures for this breakdown are available. From the mid 1980s, male employment rates for the main working age groups 25 to 34 and 35 to 49 were fairly stable. For men aged 50 to 64 the falls in the employment rate discussed above continued, falling to a low of 66.7 per cent between 1990–94, but there has been a recovery to 70.3 per cent between 2000–04. On the other hand, the employment rate has declined sharply for younger age groups; between 1985–89 and 2000–04 the rate for 16 to 17 year old males fell from 52.6 per cent to 40.7 per cent and for 18 to 24 year olds, from 74.7 per cent to 69.5 per cent. These falls follow at least in part from greatly increased participation in further and higher education.

Employment rates for female workers in all age groups above and including 25 to 34 year olds have increased substantially. The greatest increase was in the employment rate for 25 to 34 year olds, which grew from 58.3 per cent between 1985–89 to 71.6 per cent between 2000–04. There have also been substantial falls in female employment rates at younger ages, although not to as great an extent as for men.

Figure 3.6 focuses more closely on trends for the older age groups on either side of the SPA. In the most recent years employment rates for both men and women in these age groups have increased to their highest level since 1984.

Bringing together the official estimates and research discussed above, there were large reductions in the employment rates of older men between 1971 and 1981; more recently there has been a modest degree of recovery. On the other hand between 1985 and 2004 there were

Table **3.5**

Employment rates, 1985 to 2004:[1] by sex and age

United Kingdom

Percentages

	16–17	18–24	25–34	35–49	50 to SPA	SPA and over
Males						
1985–89	52.6	74.7	86.3	88.6	68.6	7.7
1990–94	47.8	69.6	85.3	87.6	66.7	7.9
1995–99	43.9	67.8	86.1	86.6	66.8	7.5
2000–04	40.7	69.5	88.1	88.4	70.3	7.9
Females						
1985–89	52.4	65.7	58.3	68.5	55.7	6.7
1990–94	47.9	64.0	64.7	72.6	58.9	7.8
1995–99	46.0	61.7	68.5	73.8	61.3	7.9
2000–04	43.8	63.0	71.6	75.6	65.8	8.9

1 Spring quarters of each year averaged over five-year periods from not seasonally adjusted data.

Source: Labour Force Survey, Office for National Statistics

Figure **3.6**

Employment rates for workers aged between 50 and SPA,[1] and SPA and over: by sex[2]

United Kingdom

Percentages

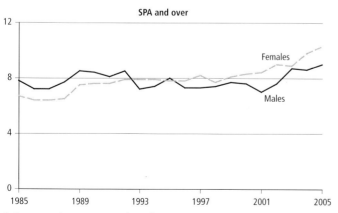

1 State pension age, currently 60 for women and 65 for men.
2 Spring quarters of each year from not seasonally adjusted data.

Source: Labour Force Survey, Office for National Statistics

reductions in employment rates for the youngest male age groups (16 to 24). Female employment has increased steadily over virtually the whole period in all age groups, except for falls in younger age groups, as for men.

The older workforce

Other data sources offer more information on the composition of this older workforce, which is of particular importance in the context of pensions.

Table 3.7 shows the composition of the older workforce in spring 2005, when the population aged 50 and above totalled 19.8 million. For men aged 50 to 64 the great majority of jobs are full time; for females jobs are allocated more evenly between full and part time. For those who stay in employment after SPA, the majority of both men and women are then in part-time employment.

Figure 3.8 shows the proportion of people in employment by industry in spring 2005 according to the 1992 Standard Industrial Classification; older workers are defined as 50 and over, and younger workers are defined as under 50. Three industries stand out as where the differences between the proportion of older and younger workers were greatest. The largest share of older workers were in public administration, education and health industries: 32 per cent, compared with 27 per cent of younger workers. The second largest share of older workers was in the distribution, hotels and restaurants category, but at 16 per cent, this was somewhat lower than the share of younger workers in these industries (21 per cent). Another sector with some difference was banking, finance

Table **3.7**

Older workers: by employment status and sex, spring 2005

United Kingdom   Percentages

	Males		Females	
	50–64	65 and over	50–59	60 and over
Economically active				
In employment				
Full-time employees	50	2	35	2
Part-time employees	5	3	27	6
Full-time self-employed	14	2	3	-
Part-time self-employed	3	2	3	1
All in employment[1]	**72**	**9**	**68**	**10**
Unemployed	2	-	2	-
All economically active	**75**	**9**	**70**	**11**
Economically inactive	**25**	**91**	**30**	**89**
All (=100%) (millions)	**5.2**	**4.0**	**3.8**	**6.8**

1 *Includes those on government-supported training and employment programmes and unpaid family workers.*

Source: Labour Force Survey, Office for National Statistics

and insurance; 14 per cent of older workers had jobs in these industries compared with 16 per cent of younger workers. More generally, while the comparison does not translate directly, the results indicate that the share of older workers in the public sector was higher than the share of younger

Figure **3.8**

Employment: by industry and age, spring 2005[1]
United Kingdom

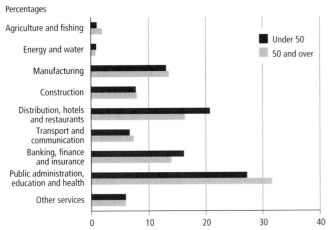

1 *Not seasonally adjusted data.*

Source: Labour Force Survey, Office for National Statistics

workers. Although normal pension age tends to be lower for public sector schemes than for private sector schemes, public sector employees appear to be more likely to stay in work until they actually reach their normal pension age.

The 2002 English Longitudinal Study of Ageing (ELSA) records a strong correlation between economic activity and non-pension wealth. The discussion here focuses on men, but the story is similar for women. ELSA defines inactivity as not being in paid work in the previous month; inactivity therefore will include most individuals who consider themselves retired and a share of the semi-retired, as well as others such as those looking after a home or family or attending formal education or training.

For men below SPA there is a relationship between wealth and retirement situation; the wealthier are more likely to report themselves as retired or semi-retired (Figure 3.9). For example, in the 55 to 59 age group, 24 per cent of those in the richest wealth quintile (see Glossary) had retired, compared with only 4 per cent of those in the poorest

Figure **3.9**

Proportion of men retired and economically inactive: by age and non-pension wealth quintile,[1] 2002
England

Percentages

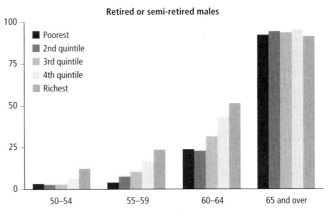

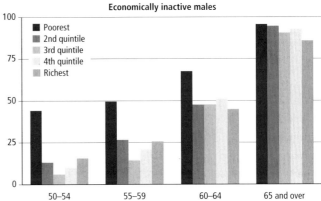

1 *See Glossary for an explanation of quintiles.*

Source: The 2002 English Longitudinal Study of Ageing

quintile. However, after SPA the share of retired people is broadly similar across each of the wealth quintiles.

Different patterns emerge from the inactivity figures. Labour market inactivity rates for men under 60 have a U-shape: both the lowest and highest wealth groups show higher levels of inactivity and those in the middle of the wealth distribution show the lowest levels of inactivity. These levels of inactivity in the lower wealth groups may in part reflect the higher levels of sickness discussed earlier. In both the 60 to 64 and 65 and over age groups the relatively higher share of inactivity among the more wealthy declines and there is evidence of an inverse relationship between wealth and inactivity, with the wealthy the least likely to be inactive.

ELSA also records interesting relationships between working patterns of older workers and their marital status. Table 3.10 shows the labour market status of individuals by age and according to marital status. The most striking feature is the higher levels of employment for married men between the ages 50 and 59. For example, for 50 to 54 year olds 69 per cent of married men were in employment compared with 46 per cent of single men; 9 per cent of single men were recorded as unemployed compared with 2 per cent of married men; and 18 per cent of single men were recorded as permanently sick compared with 6 per cent of married men. For women between ages 50 and 59, there was evidence of a similar phenomenon, but it was less striking.

Above the age of 60 these associations are less evident. Instead the main feature is the extent to which the share of single people who have retired is generally higher in all age groups than for married people. This is particularly so for women. For example 81.5 per cent of single women aged 65 and over consider themselves retired compared with 70.0 per cent of married women. However, higher numbers of married

Table **3.10**

Self-reported labour market status: by age, sex and marital status,[1] 2002

England

Percentages

	50–54		55–59		60–64		65 and over	
	Single	Married	Single	Married	Single	Married	Single	Married
Males								
Employed	45.6	68.8	40.4	57.1	29.1	34.5	1.6	2.0
Self-employed	16.1	16.4	12.5	16.1	10.7	9.8	1.6	2.3
Retired	5.7	4.9	10.4	11.9	33.1	33.6	94.7	92.9
Unemployed	9.0	2.1	9.1	2.7	3.2	3.7	0.1	0.0
Permanently sick	18.2	5.8	24.8	9.4	21.1	15.4	1.3	1.0
Other[2]	5.4	2.0	2.9	2.9	2.9	3.0	0.6	1.7
Females								
Employed	61.3	64.8	51.2	51.8	23.1	19.8	1.3	2.9
Self-employed	5.1	7.6	5.1	4.7	4.6	2.4	0.6	1.1
Retired	3.2	3.0	13.1	10.3	59.5	53.5	81.5	70.0
Unemployed	4.0	0.9	3.3	0.1	0.0	0.0	0.0	0.0
Permanently sick	20.0	4.4	17.5	9.4	3.9	3.6	3.6	3.0
Other[2]	6.4	19.3	9.8	23.7	8.9	20.8	13.0	23.1
All								
Employed	54.6	66.8	46.1	54.4	25.5	27.4	1.4	2.7
Self-employed	9.8	12.1	8.6	10.4	7.1	6.2	0.9	2.2
Retired	4.3	4.0	11.9	11.1	48.8	43.3	85.0	81.7
Unemployed	6.1	1.5	6.0	1.4	1.3	1.9	0.0	0.0
Permanently sick	19.2	5.1	20.9	9.4	10.9	9.6	3.0	2.1
Other[2]	6.0	10.5	6.5	13.3	6.5	11.7	9.7	11.5

1 Married includes married people and those who live as married.
2 Includes students, carers and people looking after the home or family.

Source: The 2002 English Longitudinal Study of Ageing

women include themselves in the 'other' category, mostly reporting themselves as 'looking after home or family'.

Retirement

From the perspective of retirement, the ELSA results in Table 3.10 illustrate the extent to which men and women retire before SPA. For men, around 5 per cent of 50 to 54 year olds, around 10 per cent of 55 to 59 year olds and around 33 per cent of 60 to 64 year olds considered themselves retired. For women, around 3 per cent of 50 to 54 year olds and 11 per cent of 55 to 59 year olds considered themselves retired. The share of women who have retired in the five years before their SPA was therefore considerably lower than the share of men who considered themselves retired in the five years before their SPA. Even taking into account the larger proportion of women in the 'other' category, the proportion of women in employment in the five years before SPA is well above that of men.

Other studies of retirement echo these results. A Department for Work and Pensions study of people aged 50 to 69 who are fully retired indicated that 59 per cent retired before SPA; the respective figures for men and women were 75 per cent and 49 per cent (Table 3.11). Factors that influenced retirement age included:

- having a private pension income; 63 per cent of those with private pension income retired before SPA compared with 55 per cent of those without;

- having a health problem; 63 per cent of those with a health problem retired before SPA compared with 52 per cent of those without;

- having a higher education qualification; 64 per cent of graduates retired before SPA compared with 53 per cent of people with no qualifications – this might suggest that wealth considerations outweigh job satisfaction considerations.

ELSA also includes a discussion of the importance of private pension provision in early retirement decisions. In total, around a third of those who retire before the normal retirement age (for their pension plan) reported that they were offered reasonable financial terms to do so. Figure 3.12 shows that among men with private pensions, there were also differences according to the type of pension held. The most likely to be retired were those with defined benefit schemes (see Glossary); among all ages from 50 to 64, the proportion of defined benefit scheme pension holders who were retired was over three times that of defined contribution pension holders.

Retirement expectations are discussed in chapter 5. The results are not directly comparable with these outturn figures because the available data uses age bands to 65 rather than to the SPA.

Table **3.11**

Retirement age relative to state pension age (SPA),[1] 2002

United Kingdom   Percentages

	Before SPA	At SPA	After SPA	Don't know	Total
All	59	26	9	6	100
Men	75	18	3	4	100
Women	49	31	14	7	100
Highest education					
Degree/other higher education	64	22	7	7	100
Other non-degree	65	21	10	4	100
No qualifications	53	30	9	7	100
Receives private pension income					
Yes	63	24	9	3	100
No	55	27	9	9	100
Has health problem					
Yes	63	22	8	7	100
No	52	33	12	4	100

1 Base: all fully retired.

Source: Factors affecting the labour market participation of older workers, Department for Work and Pensions

Figure **3.12**

**Proportion of men with private pensions who are
retired or semi-retired: by age and private pension
type, 2002**

England

Percentages

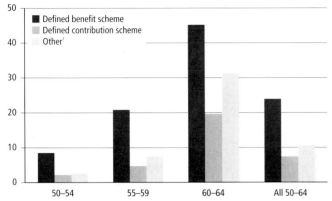

1 *Includes people who have contributed both to a defined benefit and a
defined contribution pension and those who do not know the type of
pension they are contributing to or have ever contributed to.*

Source: The 2002 English Longitudinal Study of Ageing

Sources and further reading

Coleman D and Salt J (1992) *The British Population: Patterns, Trends,
and Processes,* Oxford University Press.

Humphrey A, Costigan P, Pickering K, Stratford N and Barnes M
(2003) *Factors affecting the labour market participation of older
workers,* Department for Work and Pensions.

Marmot M, Banks J, Blundell R, Lessof C and Nazroo J (Editors) (2003)
*Health, wealth and lifestyles of the older population in England: The
2002 English Longitudinal Study of Ageing,* Institute for Fiscal Studies.

Office for National Statistics (2005) *Focus on Older People.*

Office for National Statistics, Labour Force Survey.

Pensioner income and expenditure

- Incomes of recently retired pensioners were 43 per cent higher than those where the head of the household was over 75 in 2003/04.

- Average gross incomes in 2003/04 were £244 a week for single male pensioners and £197 a week for single female pensioners. The lower non-state pension income of women accounted for much of the difference.

- Around 62 per cent of pensioner households received occupational pension income in 2003/04 and around 11 per cent received personal pension income.

- Across all pensioner households, the average level of gross income from occupational and personal pensions rose in real terms from £23 per week (at 2003/04 prices) in 1979 to £88 per week in 2003/04.

- 72 per cent of pensioner households had income from investment in 2003/04, but many only received a small amount with the median being £4 a week.

- Expenditure was lowest in households aged 75 and over, at £183 a week in 2003/04..

Chapter 4

This chapter examines the income and expenditure of people who are above the state pension age (see Glossary). Although the majority of these people are likely to have retired, a significant number continue to work on a full-time or part-time basis, see chapter 3.

The income discussed in this chapter is that of either single pensioners or couples where the man is over the state pension age. Some pensioners live in households that also include other adults, but the income of those other members is not considered here. In 2003/04 there were 25 million households in Great Britain, 7 million of which included pensioners. This estimate of pensioner households excludes 0.25 million pensioners living in institutions such as care homes. The majority of pensioner households (4.2 million) were single person households and most of these were single female pensioners (3.2 million).

Pensioner households where the head of the household is less than five years over state pension age are described as 'recently retired'. This younger group are most likely to still be in employment; estimates from the 2003/04 Family Resources Survey show that 19 per cent of recently retired single pensioners were in employment compared with 5 per cent of all single pensioners. For pensioner couples, 7 per cent of recently retired couples were both in employment compared with 3 per cent of all pensioner couples. In 29 per cent of recently retired pensioner couple households, one or both members of the couple were in employment, compared with 15 per cent of all pensioner couples.

Figure **4.1**

Gross income of pensioners:[1] by age of head of household, 2003/04

Great Britain

£ per week

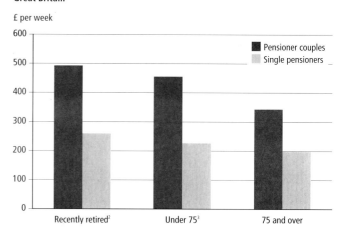

1 Pensioner couples and single pensioners.
2 Women aged 60 to 64 and men aged 65 to 69.
3 Includes the recently retired.

Source: The Pensioners' Incomes Series 2003/04, Department for Work and Pensions

Income

Figure 4.1 shows that the average gross income of pensioner households in 2003/04 declined with the age of the head of household. Incomes of recently retired pensioner couples were 43 per cent higher than the group where the head of household was over 75.

Overall, the average gross incomes of pensioner households increased in real terms from £145 per week (at 2003/04 prices)

Figure **4.2**

Gross income of pensioner households

United Kingdom/Great Britain

£ per week at 2003/04 prices

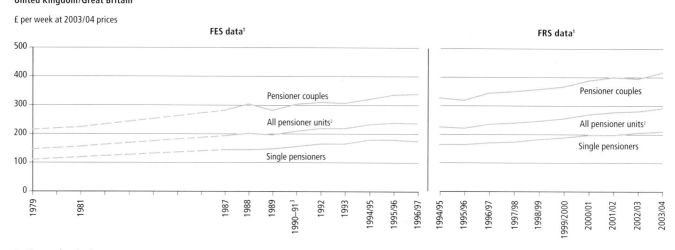

1 Figures for the l
   Expe
   The estima
2 Pensioner 'units' are defined as either single pensioners or couples where the man is over the state pension age.
3 Combined years.

Source: The Pensioners' Incomes Series 2003/04, Department for Work and Pensions

in 1979 to £291 per week in 2003/04 (Figure 4.2). In considering this rise, it should be noted that the figures are not wholly comparable. The proportion of pensioner couples within the total number of pensioner households has risen in recent years. On average, pensioner couples have higher incomes than single pensioners and a small part of the growth in pensioner household incomes since 1979 has been due to this change in the structure of pensioner households. A larger part of the growth reflects changes in sources of income, which result from the different life and work experiences of successive generations.

Average gross pensioner incomes doubled in real terms between 1979 and 2003/04, compared with average earnings across the economy as a whole, which rose by about 54 per cent over the same period. Over the more recent period between 1994/95 and 2003/04, the increase for pensioners was 29 per cent in real terms, compared with 15 per cent for average earnings.

Figure **4.3**

Median net income for pensioner couples and single pensioners, 1994/95 and 2003/04: by income quintile[1]
United Kingdom

£ per week, 2003/04 prices

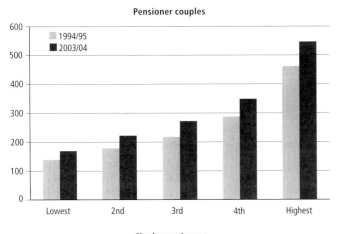

Pensioner couples

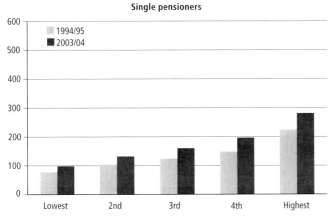

Single pensioners

1 *Calculated on net income before housing costs. See Glossary for explanation of quintile.*

Source: The Pensioners' Incomes Series 2003/04, Department for Work and Pensions

When looking at income distributions, comparisons are most commonly made on the basis of the differences between income quintiles (see Glossary). Figure 4.3 shows median net income by income quintile for pensioner couples and single pensioners in 1994/95 and 2003/04. Net income estimates provide a more consistent measure of relative standards of living than gross income.

For both pensioner couples and single pensioners, the percentage increase in median income between 1994/95 and 2003/04 was broadly comparable across all quintile groups, though increases in the middle quintiles were higher than for the lowest and highest quintiles. The middle and upper pensioner couple quintiles are more likely to include those couples where the woman is under state pension age and in work. In 2003/04, the median net income for pensioner couples in the lowest quintile was 22 per cent higher than in 1994/95, while for those in the highest quintile the increase was 18 per cent. For single pensioners, comparable increases were 25 per cent and 26 per cent respectively.

Sources of income

The income of pensioner households may be derived from various sources: state retirement pension and state benefits, private pensions, employment income, and income from investments.

The main income source for all age groups is the state retirement pension and other state benefits, including pension credit, disability benefits, housing benefit and council tax benefit (Table 4.4). The older the age group, the greater the importance of this source as older pensioners have less income from sources such as earnings. There were also differences between types of pensioner households. Single female pensioners were the most dependent on the state retirement pension and state benefits; 65 per cent of their total income came from state retirement pension and state benefits, compared with 52 per cent for single male pensioners and 42 per cent for pensioner couples, see Figure 4.6.

Income from private pensions is a significant source of income for many pensioner households, 68 per cent of whom received some private pension income in 2003/04. Private pensions include occupational pensions, personal pensions, and some earlier superannuation and annuity schemes. There was a marked increase in occupational pension provision by employers in the 1950s and 1960s and many of these employees are now retired. Because many occupational pensions are dependent on length of service, younger pensioners had greater opportunity to build up pension entitlement and the value of pension they receive is generally higher than for older pensioners.

Table **4.4**

Gross income of pensioner couples and single pensioners: by age of head of household and source of income, 2003/04

Great Britain

£ per week (percentages)

	Pensioner couples			Single pensioners		
	Recently retired[1]	Where head is under 75[2]	Where head is 75 and over	Recently retired[3]	Under 75[2]	75 and over
Gross income	**493** *(100)*	**456** *(100)*	**344** *(100)*	**260** *(100)*	**227** *(100)*	**198** *(100)*
of which:						
State pension and benefits	171 *(35)*	173 *(38)*	181 *(53)*	123 *(47)*	125 *(55)*	133 *(67)*
Occupational pension	136 *(28)*	136 *(30)*	113 *(33)*	61 *(24)*	54 *(24)*	44 *(22)*
Personal pension income	24 *(5)*	19 *(4)*	8 *(2)*	7 *(3)*	6 *(3)*	2 *(1)*
Investment income	57 *(11)*	50 *(11)*	31 *(9)*	19 *(7)*	18 *(8)*	15 *(8)*
Earnings	100 *(20)*	73 *(16)*	8 *(2)*	46 *(18)*	21 *(9)*	2 *(1)*
Other income	5 *(1)*	4 *(1)*	3 *(1)*	5 *(2)*	3 *(1)*	3 *(1)*

1 Couples where the man is aged 65 to 69.
2 Includes the recently retired.
3 Women aged 60 to 64 and men aged 65 to 69.

Source: The Pensioners' Incomes Series 2003/04, Department for Work and Pensions

The average level of gross income from occupational and personal pensions within pensioner households rose in real terms from £23 per week (at 2003/04 prices) in 1979 to £88 per week in 2003/04, increasing from 16 per cent to 30 per cent of gross income over the period (Figure 4.5).

Personal pensions are a more recent development than occupational pensions, having been introduced in 1988, and this is reflected in the figures for the receipt of private pension

income. Some 62 per cent of pensioner households received occupational pension income in 2003/04 and half of these households received less than £76 per week, whereas only 11 per cent of pensioner households received personal pension income and half of these received less than £31 per week.

The lower private pensions of women account for much of the difference in income level between men and women. In 2003/04 single male pensioners received average gross

Figure **4.5**

Occupational and personal pension income in pensioner households

United Kingdom/Great Britain

£ per week at 2003/04 prices

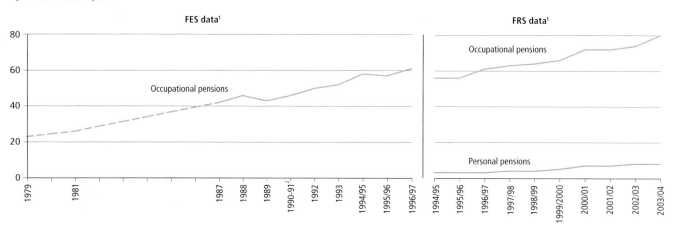

1 Figures for the last ten years are based on the Family Resources Survey (FRS), which covers Great Britain. Early figures are based on the Family Expenditure Survey (FES), which covers the United Kingdom. Figures between 1979 and 1981, and 1981 and 1987 have been interpolated. The estimates from the two sources are not directly comparable so figures for 1994/95 and the following two years are shown on both bases.
2 Combined years.

Source: The Pensioners' Incomes Series 2003/04, Department for Work and Pensions

Figure 4.6

Average gross weekly income of single pensioners: by sex and source, 2003/04

Great Britain

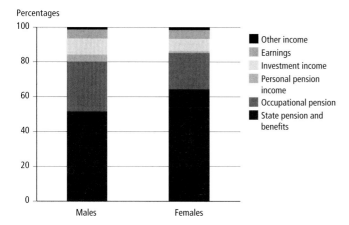

Total income: £244 (males), £197 (females)

Source: The Pensioners' Incomes Series 2003/04, Department for Work and Pensions

incomes of £244 per week, £80 of which came from private pensions, while single female pensioners received £197 per week, only £43 of which came from private pensions (Figure 4.6).

There are a number of reasons for this difference. Women generally have less opportunity to build up pension entitlement during their working life, because of lower pay and greater likelihood of discontinuities in their employment history. Single female pensioners are generally older than single male pensioners and the value of a private pension tends to be lower for people who have been retired longer. One of the reasons for this decline is that average earnings have increased more quickly than prices with the result that newly retired pensioners with salary-related pensions will generally receive a higher pension than someone in an equivalent job who had retired several years earlier with the same pension entitlement. A further reason for the decline in the real value of pension income over time is that over two thirds of pension annuities are flat-rate and do not increase in level over time. Finally, a high proportion of single female pensioners are widows. The level of occupational pension received by a widow is generally only half the level of the pension received by the couple when the man was alive.

Looking briefly at the other main sources, 20 per cent of the income of newly retired pensioner couples came from employment in 2003/04, but for couples where the head of household was aged 75 and over, only 2 per cent of the couple's income came from this source, see Table 4.4. The figures were slightly lower for single pensioners, falling from 18 per cent for newly retired pensioners to 1 per cent for those aged 75 and over.

A high proportion (72 per cent in 2003/04) of pensioner households has some investment income, but most receive only a small amount. The median amount received across all pensioner households was £4 per week in 2003/04. The proportion receiving some investment income was higher for pensioner couples (77 per cent) than for single pensioners (64 per cent).

Expenditure

Patterns of expenditure change with age. Expenditure was lowest for those households where the household reference person (see Glossary) was aged 75 or over, £183 per week in 2003/04 (Table 4.7). This is in part explained by the lower proportion of couples in this older age group. These households have on average 1.4 persons compared with an average 2.2 persons in households where the reference person was aged 50 to 64, or 1.7 persons in households of the 65 to 74 age group. The major expenditure items for the oldest households were food (16 per cent), housing, including council tax (13 per cent) and recreation (12 per cent). The expenditure in pre-retirement and newly retired households, where the reference person was aged 50 to 64, was much higher, £441.30 per week. The major expenditure items were transport and recreation (both 15 per cent) followed by housing, including council tax (13 per cent) and food (11 per cent).

Categories where the proportion – though not necessarily the amount – of expenditure rose with age included food, fuel, power and water, and health. The proportion of expenditure on transport and restaurants and hotels fell with age. Transport includes both purchase and maintenance of vehicles and public transport costs. It might be expected to be lower as the oldest pensioners would be least likely to have travel to work costs. Housing costs were lower for the age groups over 50 than the younger ages; within the housing category, the proportion of expenditure on council tax and on repair and maintenance rose while that on mortgage interest and rent (net of benefit) generally fell. This reflects changes in the proportion of households with a mortgage at various ages – overall, some two thirds of households headed by pensioners own their house outright.

There is some evidence that lower consumption on all types of expenditure arises from the constraints imposed by lack of mobility or ill health as well as from lower incomes or choice. Figure 4.8 illustrates how the difficulty of accessing local amenities rises with age. Over 20 per cent of men aged 80 and over have difficulty in getting to a bank or shopping centre. For women aged 80 and over, nearly 30 per cent have difficulty in getting to these facilities and over 20 per cent even to local shops or a post office.

Table 4.7

Weekly household expenditure: by age of household reference person,[1] 2003/04

United Kingdom   Percentages

	Under 30	30–49	50–64	65–74	75 and over	All households
Food and non-alcoholic drinks	8	10	11	13	16	10
Alcoholic drinks, tobacco and narcotics	3	3	3	3	3	3
Clothing and footwear	6	6	5	4	4	5
Housing	20	16	13	11	13	15
of which:						
Mortgage interest and net rent	16	12	6	3	4	9
Council tax	3	3	4	5	6	4
Repair and maintenance	1	2	2	3	3	2
Fuel, power and water	3	3	4	5	7	4
Household goods and services	7	7	7	9	8	7
Health	1	1	2	2	3	1
Transport	15	15	15	12	11	15
Communication	3	3	3	2	3	3
Recreation and culture	11	13	15	16	12	14
Education	1	2	1	–	–	1
Restaurants and hotels	9	9	8	7	6	8
Miscellaneous goods and services	8	8	8	8	10	8
Other expenditure items	4	5	5	6	5	5
All household expenditure (=100%) (£ per week)	**408.40**	**524.80**	**441.30**	**289.60**	**183.30**	**418.10**
Average expenditure per person (£ per week)	178.00	175.90	198.30	173.00	127.40	177.40
Weighted average household size (number of persons)	2.3	3.0	2.2	1.7	1.4	2.4

1 See Glossary for an explanation of household reference person.

Source: Family Spending 2003/04, Office for National Statistics

Figure 4.8

Proportion of men and women with difficulty in accessing local amenities: by selected age groups

England

Percentages

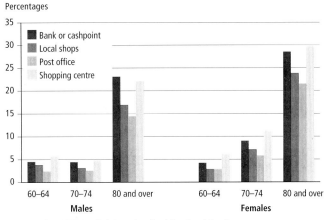

Source: The 2002 English Longitudinal Study of Ageing

The oldest pensioners may spend less of their gross income than younger households. Analysis based on the Expenditure and Food Survey for 2002/03 suggests that the group aged over 70 spent 76 per cent compared with 92 per cent where the reference person was aged 50 to 64 and 90 per cent where the reference person was aged 65 to 69. However these figures are based on expenditure levels over two weeks and income over a longer period and do not include other sources such as savings, so may not entirely reflect the overall position.

Sources and further reading

Department for Work and Pensions, *The Pensioners' Incomes Series 2003/04*.

Marmot M, Banks J, Blundell R, Lessof C and Nazroo J (Editors), (2003) *Health, wealth and lifestyles of the older population in England: The 2002 English Longitudinal Study of Ageing*, The Institute for Fiscal Studies.

Office for National Statistics, *Family Spending 2003/04*.

Attitudes to retirement and pension planning

- In 2002, 34 per cent of working-age people in work or intending to be in work in the near future expected to retire at 60; 24 per cent expected to retire before 60 and 34 per cent after 60.

- Self-employed people were more likely than employees to anticipate working after state pension age.

- 56 per cent of working-age people in Great Britain expected their retirement to last at least 20 years. Only 7 per cent thought they would be in retirement for less than ten years.

- In 2002, 52 per cent of people of working age thought a weekly income of less than £250 would be adequate to live on if they retired today.

- Almost four in ten individuals thought that an adequate retirement income would be less than their current income, and almost two in ten thought that it would be more.

- Almost two thirds of people agree that putting money into a pension is the most secure way of saving for retirement.

This chapter examines the extent that people plan for retirement, and what their expectations are. It includes the age at which they expect to retire, the sources of income they expect to have when they do retire, and their attitudes to pensions and savings.

People often delay pension planning until later in life. The British Household Panel survey shows that the proportion of people who say they are saving specifically for their old age rises steeply when people reach their mid 40s. There are a number of reasons for this delay, which include:

- an unwillingness or inability to grapple with complex financial matters surrounding pensions;

- a reluctance to deal with uncomfortable notions of retirement and old age;

- a perception that retirement is a long way off and planning for it is less pressing than other, more immediate, financial commitments; and

- a lack of clarity about what the future may bring and about retirement and retirement income.

A combination of factors, including attitudes, may determine the extent that people save for retirement. Whether individuals believe that they should take responsibility for their own retirement, whether they are regular savers, and their financial ability and practical opportunity to save, could affect the decisions they take about retirement saving.

Expected age of retirement

People's expectations of when they might retire may not match when they actually do so, but these expectations may affect the decisions they make during their working lives about saving and planning for retirement. Pensions 2002, a survey of public attitudes to pensions and saving for retirement, found that 34 per cent of working-age people in work or intending to be in work in the near future expected to retire at 60 (Figure 5.1). However, 24 per cent of people expected to retire before this age and a further 34 per cent after this age, with the majority (27 per cent) at 65.

The pattern is slightly different between men and women, reflecting the difference in state pension age (SPA, see Glossary). In both cases a substantial minority expected to retire at their respective SPA: 42 per cent of women expected to retire at 60 (and 25 per cent of men), while 35 per cent of men expected to retire at 65 (and 18 per cent of women).

Overall, 52 per cent of men and 69 per cent of women of working age in work or intending to be in work in the future expected to retire before the age of 65 (Figure 5.2). Women in

Figure 5.1

Expected age of retirement of working-age people:[1] by sex, 2002

Great Britain

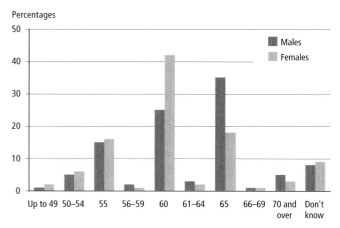

1 Those in work or intending to be in work in the future.

Source: **Pensions 2002: Public attitudes to pensions and saving for retirement,** *Department for Work and Pensions*

all age groups were more likely than men to anticipate retiring before 65, despite their SPA being gradually increased from 60 to 65 over the period 2010 to 2020. This suggests that they might be unaware of this forthcoming change, or that if they are aware, it does not affect the age at which they plan to retire. To put these figures into context, the actual proportions still economically active in 2004 were 56 per cent of men aged 60 to 64 and 30 per cent of women. Trends in employment and retirement are discussed in chapter 3.

Self-employed people were more likely to expect to continue working into their 60s, and people with experience of

Figure 5.2

Working-age people[1] expecting to retire before 65: by sex and age, 2002

Great Britain

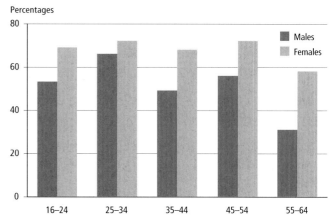

1 Those in work or intending to be in work in the future.

Source: **Pensions 2002: Public attitudes to pensions and saving for retirement,** *Department for Work and Pensions*

self-employment during their working lives were more likely to expect to work after SPA than employees. Only 2 per cent of employees expected to work to at least 70 compared with 14 per cent of the self-employed, and 36 per cent of employees expected to retire at 60 compared with only 17 per cent of the self-employed (Figure 5.3). A further 6 per cent of employees did not know when they expected to retire compared with 17 per cent of the self-employed. These expectations are in line with evidence suggesting that the self-employed tend to be an older group in the workforce; 24 per cent of self-employed workers covered in the Pensions 2002 survey were aged 55 and over compared with 14 per cent of employees.

Figure **5.3**

Expected age of retirement: by employment status, 2002

Great Britain

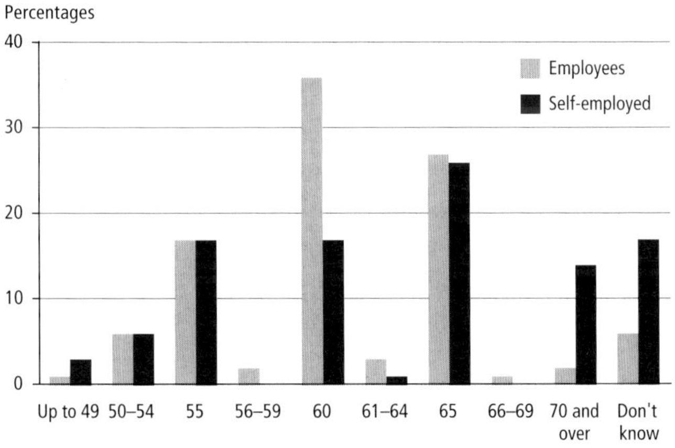

Percentages

Source: Pensions 2002: Public attitudes to pensions and saving for retirement, *Department for Work and Pensions*

Expected length of retirement

Length of retirement is determined by life expectancy and the age at which an individual retires from paid work. The longer an individual's retirement, the longer the period of time their income and wealth, which for most people is accumulated during their working life, must be spread over. This has implications for the level of pension saving that they need to make to achieve a certain standard of living.

In 2002, 15 per cent of working-age individuals in Great Britain were unable to estimate how long they would be in retirement, but over half (56 per cent) expected this to be at least 20 years. Women were more likely than men to expect a retirement of 20 or more years (62 per cent compared with 48 per cent). Only 7 per cent of individuals thought they would be in retirement for less than ten years.

The length of retirement people expected to have is linked to the age at which they expected to retire. Thus, individuals expecting to retire before SPA were more likely to anticipate a long retirement, with 33 per cent anticipating a retirement of 20 to 24 years and a further 31 per cent expecting their retirement to be 25 years or longer (Figure 5.4). Only 4 per cent of people retiring before SPA expected their retirement to last nine years or less.

Figure **5.4**

Expected length of retirement: by age expected to retire in relation to state pension age (SPA),[1] 2002

Great Britain

Percentages

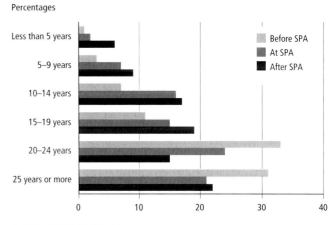

1 Excludes 'don't knows'.

Source: Pensions 2002: Public attitudes to pensions and saving for retirement, *Department for Work and Pensions*

Figures on the actual length of life after an individual's date of retirement are not available. However, Government Actuary's Department projections of cohort life expectancy (see Glossary) at SPA were 18.5 years for men aged 65 and 26.3 years for women aged 60 in 2002.

Findings from the 2002 English Longitudinal Study of Ageing (ELSA) suggest that there is a relationship between wealth and the expectation of reaching a specific age. In the 65 and under age group, for example, on average 69 per cent of the richest quintile (see Glossary) expected to reach age 75, compared with 59 per cent of the poorest quintile (Figure 5.5). For individuals aged 70 to 74 there was less variation in the average expectation of reaching age 85, ranging from 52 per cent of the richest to 48 per cent of the second poorest wealth quintile. Although there is no direct measure of the actual relationship between life expectancy and wealth, there is a well established relationship between higher social class and greater longevity, suggesting this expectation may be well founded.

Figure **5.5**

Expected mortality:[1] by age and wealth quintile,[2] 2002

England

Percentages

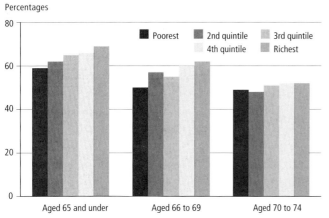

1 Expectation of living to age 75, 80 and 85, by individuals aged 65 and under, 66 to 69 and 70 to 74 respectively.
2 See Glossary for an explanation of quintile.

Source: The 2002 English Longitudinal Study of Ageing

Expected levels of retirement income

Most people find it difficult to estimate what they will need when they come to retire. Several factors can affect actual retirement income, and perceived needs may well differ from the actual needs in retirement. It is easier for people to estimate what they would consider to be an adequate retirement income if they were retired today. In 2002, 52 per cent of people of working age thought that a weekly income of up to £249 was adequate for them to live on if they were retired today (Figure 5.6). A further 29 per cent thought that

Figure **5.6**

Weekly income considered adequate to live on if retired today,[1] 2002

Great Britain

Percentages

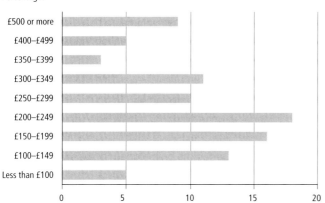

1 Excludes 'don't knows'.

Source: Pensions 2002: Public attitudes to pensions and saving for retirement, *Department for Work and Pensions*

they would need an income of between £250 and £499 a week, while 9 per cent felt that they would need an income of £500 a week or more.

Comparing current incomes with those considered enough to live on in retirement suggests that people on the lowest incomes tended to think that an adequate retirement income for them was greater than their current income. Of people earning less than £100 a week, 72 per cent thought they would need a retirement income that was more than £100 a week. People on moderate and high incomes were more likely to consider that a retirement income below their current income would be adequate. For example, 48 per cent of those earning £500 or more a week thought that a retirement income of under £400 a week would be sufficient, and 52 per cent of those earning between £400 and £499 a week thought that a retirement income of under £300 a week would be adequate.

Table **5.7**

Relationship between current income, perceived adequate retirement income and pension status, 2002

Great Britain   Percentages

	'Adequate' retirement income less than current income	'Adequate' retirement income same as current income	'Adequate' retirement income more than current income
Currently have private pension	73	56	31
Do not currently have private pension	25	35	63
of which: never had private pension	14	26	43
All (includes 'don't knows')	**100**	**100**	**100**

Source: Pensions 2002: Public attitudes to pensions and saving for retirement, *Department for Work and Pensions*

Overall, almost four in ten individuals thought that an adequate retirement income would be less than their current income, over three in ten thought it would be the same, and almost two in ten thought that it would be more than their current income. For individuals who thought that an adequate retirement income for them would be less than their current income, nearly three quarters currently had a private pension (Table 5.7). Among those who believed an adequate income would be more than their current income, only three in ten had a private pension, while over two fifths had never had a private pension.

Expected sources of income in retirement

Most people of working age (91 per cent) know what their main source of income in retirement might be. In 2002 just over three quarters (78 per cent) expected it to be pension-based, whether the state or a private (occupational, personal or stakeholder) pension, or a share of their partner's pension income (Table 5.8).

Table **5.8**

Expected main sources of retirement income, 2002

Great Britain	Percentages
Own pension	**68**
Basic state pension	20
Occupational pension	33
Personal pension	14
Stakeholder pension	1
Partner's pension	**10**
Basic state pension	1
Occupational pension	7
Personal pension	2
Non-pension	**13**
Don't know	**9**
All	**100**

Source: Pensions 2002: Public attitudes to pensions and saving for retirement, *Department for Work and Pensions*

Most of the 13 per cent of individuals who did not expect their main source of retirement income to be pension-based expected to derive income from other savings and investments such as stocks and shares (38 per cent) and property (28 per cent), mainly from renting property out but also from the profit made by selling their house and moving to somewhere smaller. A lower proportion (11 per cent) expected that their non-pension income would be from earnings from paid employment, and fewer still from state benefits (2 per cent).

Women are less likely than men to have private pensions. They are less likely to be in work and if they are, less likely to be in full-time work, so are more likely to derive income from a partner or spouse's income. Overall, 18 per cent of women expected this to be the case compared with 2 per cent of men. Across different groups of women, married women not in work were the most likely to expect their main source of retirement income to come from their partner's pension (54 per cent). Only 12 per cent of women with private pension provision expected their partner's pension to be the main source of their retirement income.

People on lower incomes were more likely to expect state pensions to form the main part of their income in retirement. For those earning up to £10,400 a year, 31 per cent expected state pensions to be their main source of income compared with just 1 per cent of those earning £31,200 and over. Over three quarters (76 per cent) of those earning £31,200 and over expected private pensions to be their main source of income in retirement.

More than half (56 per cent) of people who expected to retire before SPA expected their main source of income to derive from their own private pensions (Table 5.9). Only 9 per cent expected to rely on state pensions. In contrast 32 per cent

Table **5.9**

Main source of retirement income: by expected retirement age relative to state pension age (SPA), 2002

Great Britain   Percentages

	Retire before SPA	Retire at SPA	Retire after SPA	Don't know when will retire	Don't expect to work again
Own state pensions	9	26	32	27	52
Own private pensions	56	53	37	22	11
Partner's pensions (any type)	12	4	7	5	17
Earnings (own or partner's)	1	1	5	4	1
Social security benefits	–	.	.	.	3
Other non-pension sources	14	8	12	17	5
Don't know	8	8	6	25	11
All	**100**	**100**	**100**	**100**	**100**

Source: Pensions 2002: Public attitudes to pensions and saving for retirement, *Department for Work and Pensions*

expecting to retire after SPA expected to rely mainly on state pensions. Just over half (52 per cent) of people who did not expect to work again, thought that state pensions would be their main source of income and 3 per cent thought that state benefits would form their main source of income.

Just over two thirds of individuals currently contributing to private pensions (67 per cent) expected their main source of income in retirement to be from their own private pensions, more than twice as many as those who had a pension in the past but no longer did (29 per cent) (Table 5.10). For individuals who had never had a private pension, almost a quarter (24 per cent) expected this to be their main source of income in retirement, suggesting their intention to take one out in the future. These people are more likely to be in the younger age groups, and it is likely that they have not yet started thinking about or planning their retirement. One in ten people with private pensions expected their main retirement

income to come from a non-pension source. For those currently without or who have never had a private pension, almost one third expected that state pensions would form the major part of their retirement income. Partner's pensions (mainly private) were also more significant for these categories, with around one in seven expecting their main source of income in retirement to come from this source.

People who expected their main source of income to be their own private pensions were twice as likely to strongly agree than to strongly disagree (55 per cent compared with 27 per cent) that pensions were the most secure way of saving for retirement. Among people who strongly disagreed with this statement, there was a greater likelihood (33 per cent) of expecting that their main source of retirement income would come from a non-pensions source, such as property and other kinds of savings and investments.

Most people within ten years of their expected retirement age thought that their main source of retirement income would come from pensions. Over one half expected to derive their income mainly from private pensions and around one quarter from state pensions. Only 1 per cent expected their main source of retirement income to come from state benefits.

Table **5.10**

Expected main source of retirement income: by current pension status, 2002

Great Britain   Percentages

	Currently have private pension	Had private pension in past but do not currently have one	Never had a private pension
Own state pensions	11	30	29
Partner's state pensions	1	1	3
Own private pensions	67	29	24
Partner's private pensions	5	14	11
Property	3	8	3
Other savings and investments	5	4	4
Social security benefits	–	–	1
Own earnings from paid work	–	3	1
Partner's earnings from paid work	1	1	.
Inheritance	–	1	.
Sale of possessions	–	.	.
Income/allowance from children	.	.	1
Other	1	3	2
Don't know	4	5	20
All	**100**	**100**	**100**

Source: Pensions 2002: Public attitudes to pensions and saving for retirement, *Department for Work and Pensions*

Attitudes to pensions and saving for retirement

More working-age people in Great Britain agreed (56 per cent) than disagreed (41 per cent) with the statement that 'I find it more satisfying to spend money than to save it'.

Figure **5.11**

Attitudes towards spending and saving money:[1] by current pension status, 2002

Great Britain

Percentages

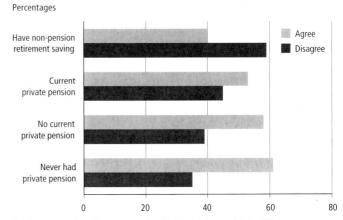

1 Agreement or disagreement with the statement 'I find it more satisfying to spend money than to save it'.

Source: Pensions 2002: Public attitudes to pensions and saving for retirement, *Department for Work and Pensions*

Those who had never had a private pension were most likely to agree with this statement (Figure 5.11). Those who currently had a private pension were also more likely to agree (53 per cent) than disagree (45 per cent) that they preferred spending money. Only people with non-pensions retirement saving, such as those with savings accounts, insurance company policies, and stocks and shares, were more likely to prefer saving money (59 per cent).

The more thought people had given to their retirement, the less likely they were to prioritise current living standards over retirement savings (Figure 5.12). Differences were most marked in people who had not thought about retirement at all; 66 per cent agreed that they would rather make sure they had a good standard of living today than save for retirement compared with 24 per cent who disagreed.

Figure **5.12**

Attitudes towards having a good standard of living rather than saving for retirement:[1] by amount of thought given to retirement, 2002

Great Britain

Percentages

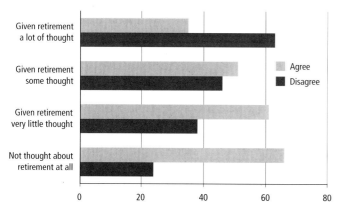

1 Agreement or disagreement with the statement 'I would rather make sure I had a good standard of living today than save for retirement'.

Source: Pensions 2002: Public attitudes to pensions and saving for retirement, *Department for Work and Pensions*

Almost two thirds (65 per cent) agreed with the statement 'Putting money into a pension is the most secure way of saving for retirement', which sought to explore the extent to which people had confidence in pensions. Just under three in ten (29 per cent) disagreed with the statement (Figure 5.13).

The type of pension provision made little difference to people's attitudes; 65 per cent of those who had never had a private pension thought that pensions were secure, while 33 per cent of those who currently had a private pension did not think they were. More employees (66 per cent) than the

Figure **5.13**

Attitudes towards putting money into a pension as the most secure way of saving for retirement:[1] by current pension status, 2002

Great Britain

Percentages

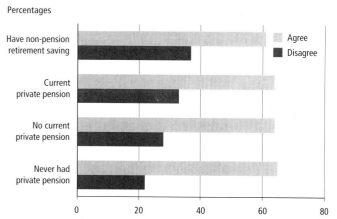

1 Agreement or disagreement with the statement 'Putting money into a pension is the most secure way of saving for retirement'.

Source: Pensions 2002: Public attitudes to pensions and saving for retirement, *Department for Work and Pensions*

self-employed (52 per cent) thought that pensions were secure, and a greater number of the self-employed (45 per cent) than employees (29 per cent) thought that they were not.

Sources and further reading

Hedges A (1998) *Pensions and retirement planning,* Department for Social Security Research Report No. 83.

Mayhew V (2003) *Pensions 2002: Public attitudes to pensions and saving for retirement,* Department for Work and Pensions Research Report No. 193. Covers working-age individuals (aged 16 and over).

McKay S and Kempson E (2003) *Savings and life events,* Department for Work and Pensions Research Report No. 194. Incorporates analysis of the British Household Panel survey.

State pension entitlements and second tier pension provision

- 11.4 million pensioners received basic state retirement pension, the main state pension payment, in September 2004.

- In 2002/03, 32.1 million people gained a qualifying year's entitlement for the basic state pension, 20.3 million by paying National Insurance contributions.

- Men currently aged 40 to 44 have built up fewer qualifying years towards the basic state pension than men in earlier age cohorts had when they were aged 40 to 44. For women the opposite is true.

- There were 12.1 million male employees with second tier pension provision in 2002/03; 5.3 million of these were in the state second pension compared with 2.9 million in 1992/93.

- 3.1 million women had no second tier pension provision in 2002/03, compared with 5.6 million in 1978/79.

This chapter is the first of several dealing with future pensioners and the ways in which people save for retirement. It covers state pensions and alternative ways in which individuals can build up additional 'second tier' entitlements (see Glossary).

The analyses of pensioner income in chapter 4 show that for many pensioners the state retirement pension is their main source of income in retirement. Although people think of the state retirement pension as a single payment, it is made up of a number of different elements. There are four main components: basic state pension, graduated pension benefit, additional pension from the state earnings-related pension system, and state second pension. The amount of pension that an individual will receive for each of these components will depend upon their age, marital status, employment history, private pension status and income.

Table 6.1 shows the average state retirement pension payment in September 2004, together with the average value of the four main components. Basic state retirement pension is the main payment, paid to 11.4 million pensioners in September 2004. Not all of these pensioners received the full amount (£82.05 per week in 2005/06) as entitlement varies with the number of qualifying years of National Insurance (NI) contributions or credits that an individual has built up; the number of years for which Home Responsibilities Protection was awarded; and the length of the individual's working life (see box).

Graduated retirement benefit is a supplementary pension based on the number of graduated pension units built up by an employee. Graduated pension was replaced in 1978 by the state earnings-related pension system (SERPS), so only individuals in work before 1978 will have entitlement to graduated pension benefit. Contributions paid through SERPS provide entitlement to earnings-related additional pension payments. State second pension (S2P) replaced SERPS in April 2002, so recently retired individuals will have built up a small amount of S2P pension entitlement, but those who retired before April 2002 will have no S2P pension.

Basic state pension

This section concentrates on the ways that individuals are building up entitlement to the basic state pension and the level of their entitlements. In 2002/03, there were 32.1 million people who gained a qualifying year for the basic state pension. The majority of these (20.3 million) paid NI contributions for the full year. A further 4.7 million people gained a qualifying year through credits, and an additional 2.5 million, mainly women, gained Home Responsibilities Protection. The remaining 4.6 million gained a qualifying year through a combination of contributions and credits.

Figure 6.2 shows the number of people paying NI contributions for the years 1978/79 to 2002/03 by category of contribution. Class 1 contributions are paid by the employed and Class 2 contributions by the self-employed, who do not build up entitlement to SERPS or S2P. The number of men paying Class 2 contributions increased from 1.2 million in 1978/79 to 1.9 million in 1989/90, but has since declined and in 2002/03 there were 1.6 million men paying Class 2 contributions.

In 1978/79 there were 6.1 million male employees paying Class 1 contributions at the not contracted out rate (see box) and building up entitlement to SERPS. The number of men paying this class of contribution rose slightly in 1979/80 to

Table **6.1**

Average state retirement pension: by category of payment, sex and age of recipient, 2004[1]

Great Britain

£ per week

	Males		Females		All	
	Under 80	80 and over	Under 80	80 and over	Under 80	80 and over
Average rate of state retirement pension[2]	**100.87**	**89.83**	**69.27**	**76.58**	**81.47**	**81.07**
of which:						
Basic state pension	73.90	74.71	57.73	70.04	63.97	71.62
Graduated retirement benefit	4.09	3.80	1.17	1.66	2.30	2.39
State earnings-related pension	21.66	9.46	9.70	3.33	14.32	5.40
Second state pension	0.17	0.00	0.10	0.00	0.13	0.00

1 At 30 September.
2 Includes, in addition to the four listed components, small amounts of age allowance, invalidity allowance, adult dependency increment and child dependency increment.

Source: Department for Work and Pensions

6.2 million, but numbers fluctuated during the 1980s. The most marked trend has been the steady increase from 6.3 million in 1992/93 to 8.8 million in 2002/03. In 1978/79 there were 6.9 million male employees who were members of private pension schemes and paying NI contributions at the contracted out rate. Since then, numbers have generally declined and in 2002/03 there were only 3.7 million male employees paying contracted out rate contributions.

The trends are slightly different for women. The most marked trend is the decline in the number of female employees paying married women's reduced rate contributions, from 3.6 million in 1978/79 to 93,000 in 2002/03. Reduced rate contributions do not give entitlement to state pension. The option to choose reduced rate contributions was withdrawn in April 1978, but married women who were paying these contributions were allowed to continue on this basis. The decline in reduced rate

State pension entitlement, National Insurance and qualifying years

All employees earning above a specified weekly earnings threshold pay National Insurance (NI) contributions. A tax year is counted as a 'qualifying year' towards the basic state pension provided the employee has earnings above the weekly threshold, pays NI contributions during the year and has annual earnings that exceed the value of the weekly threshold multiplied by 52.

To receive a full basic state retirement pension, an individual must have made paid contributions or received credits for the required number of qualifying years (currently 44 for men and 39 for women). The state pension age for women will increase gradually from 60 to 65 between 2010 and 2020, and during this period the number of qualifying years for a woman will also increase from 39 to 44.

Where individuals are unable to work because they care for a child or a sick or disabled person, the number of qualifying years that they need is reduced by means of the Home Responsibilities Protection (HRP). The number of HRP years is capped and to receive the full basic state pension, individuals must have at least 20 non-HRP qualifying years (22 from 2020).

A reduced state retirement pension is paid if an individual does not have the required number of qualifying years. The value of the pension received is proportionate to the actual number of qualifying years relative to the required number. No state retirement pension is paid where an individual has less than a quarter of the required qualifying years (currently 11 for men and 10 for women).

Women who were paying 'married woman's' reduced rate NI contributions in 1978 retained the right to continue to pay reduced rate contributions. These women do not build up pension entitlements and their pension will be dependent on their husband's NI contributions.

Supplementary pensions

Employees who pay NI contributions at the standard rate build up entitlements to an earnings-related pension paid as a supplement to the basic state pension. The value of the supplementary pension depends upon the number of qualifying years and the value of NI contributions paid. The current earnings-related pension scheme, the state second pension (S2P), was introduced in 2002 and replaced the state earnings-related pension scheme (SERPS), which had in turn replaced the graduated pension scheme in 1978. An employee reaching state pension age in 2005 could receive basic state pension plus payments from each of these three supplementary pensions.

Since 1978 members of an occupational pension scheme that meets certain requirements, in terms of the level of contributions and benefits, are considered to have adequate private pension provision and the pension scheme can 'contract out' of the supplementary state pension scheme. Contracting out means that employers and employees pay a lower rate of NI contributions, and the employees build up entitlement to the basic state pension but their entitlement to S2P is reduced.

Since 1988 it has also been possible to contract out by means of a personal pension. The holder pays NI contributions at the standard contracted in rate, but a NI rebate, reflecting the difference between the contracted in and contracted out rate, is paid into their personal pension on an annual basis as an addition to other contributions. From 2001 contracted out stakeholder pensions were introduced as an alternative to a personal pension.

Self-employment

Self-employed individuals pay a lower rate of NI contribution and build up entitlement to the basic state pension, but are excluded from SERPS and S2P.

Figure **6.2**

Number of people paying National Insurance contributions:[1] by type of contribution

United Kingdom

Millions

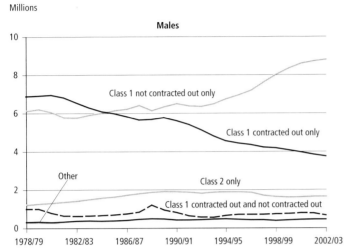

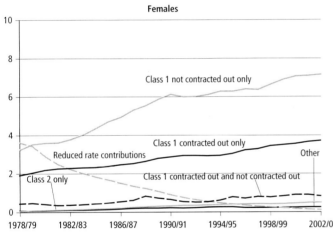

1 *Figures for 2001/02 and 2002/03 should be regarded as provisional and may be subject to changes in future releases.*

Source: Department for Work and Pensions

contributions has been offset by increases in Class 1 contributions, both contracted out and not contracted out.

The number of female employees paying Class 1 contributions at the contracted out rate increased from 1.9 million in 1978/79 to 3.7 million in 2002/03. Over the same period the number of female employees paying Class 1 contributions at the not contracted out rate increased from 3.2 million to 7.1 million. The number of women making any contributions increased from 9.2 million in 1978/79 to 12.4 million in 2002/03, reflecting the changes in the employment rates for women described in chapter 3.

Age cohorts

The number of qualifying years for basic state pension built up by an individual will depend upon their employment history

and the length of their working life. Analyses at the aggregate level can mask the variation between different groups. Changes in employment rates and patterns over the last 30 years mean that the typical employment pattern for an individual currently aged 30 to 34 may be different from that of an individual who was aged 30 to 34 in the 1980s or 1970s. One way of exploring these changes is to study age generation groups (or cohorts), for example taking those aged 50 to 54 in 2002/03 and looking back across the years to see how much state pension they had built up when they were aged 40 to 44, and comparing their histories with the group of individuals who are currently age 40 to 44.

Figure 6.3 presents information for different age bands, with the lines showing the pension histories of different age cohorts. It shows the variation in the number of qualifying years that men and women of different age cohorts have built up at specific ages. Looking at the male chart, the topmost line shows information for those aged 60 to 64 in 2002/03, starting with the number of qualifying years that these men had built up 25 years ago when they were aged 35 to 39, then following them through to age 60 to 64. The other lines present the same information for younger age groups. All data relate to the 25th percentile: one quarter of the age cohort will have qualifying years equal to this value or less, and three quarters of the age cohort will have built up this value or more qualifying years. The comparisons of age cohorts exclude those with no record on the NI system because they have never earned sufficient to pay NI contributions.

The average number of qualifying years for men has declined over the last 25 years. Of men currently aged 40 to 44 or 45 to 49, three quarters have built up 19 or more qualifying years, somewhat less then men currently aged 60 to 64, three quarters of whom had built up 23 or more years when they were aged 40 to 44. One of the differences affecting these results has been the changes in the education system. Men aged 50 and over in 2002/03 would have been able to leave school at 15, but for younger age cohorts the school leaving age was 16 and many will have stayed on until 18, so they have fewer years in employment to build up qualifying years than the older men.

The trend in the number of women building up qualifying years is different to those for men (see Figure 6.2) because of changes in employment and contribution rates. This also means that the variation in the number of qualifying years built up by different age cohorts is more marked for women than for men. The number of women excluded from the analysis because they have no record on the NI system is smaller in more recent cohorts, and taking account of this would further increase the variation between cohorts.

Figure **6.3**

Number of qualifying years for basic state pension for people currently aged 40 and over: by age cohort[1]

United Kingdom

Qualifying years

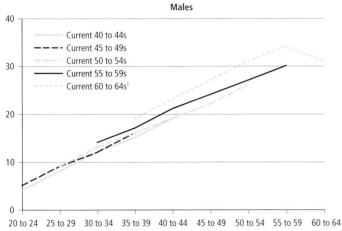

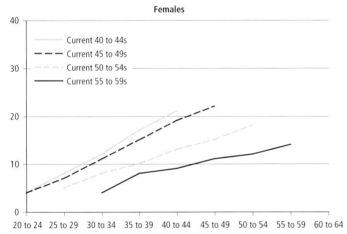

1 *25th percentile. For an explanation of percentiles see Glossary.*
2 *The apparent fall in the number of qualifying years at ages 60 to 64 is explained by a change in the composition of the cohort. The cohort of men currently aged 60 to 64 includes some men with a small number of qualifying years received only through automatic credits that are granted from the age of 60 onwards. This group is excluded from the comparisons for the younger age bands.*

Source: Department for Work and Pensions

Figure 6.3 shows that the current generations of women are building up more qualifying years towards the basic state retirement pension than earlier generations, and in retirement will be less dependent on the NI contributions of their spouse than current pensioners. One major factor accounting for the changes in pension entitlement was the removal of reduced rate contributions in 1978. However, some of the women aged over 40 in 2002/03 would have been married and paying reduced rate contributions in 1978, and have since continued to pay the reduced rate even though these contributions do not provide qualification for basic state pension.

Of women currently aged 40 to 44, three quarters had built up 21 or more qualifying years for basic state pension, slightly

more than the women currently aged 45 to 49, three quarters of whom had built up 19 or more years when they were aged 40 to 44, and markedly more than the women currently aged 55 to 59, one quarter of whom had built up 9 years or less when they were aged 40 to 44.

Second tier pension provision

To compare pension systems on an international basis, pension provision can be categorised into three 'tiers'. The UK pension system does not fit neatly into these categories but the following definitions are generally used:

- First tier – basic state retirement pension and means tested social benefits;

- Second tier – all contracted out personal and occupational pensions, and state second pension (S2P formerly SERPS), which includes all not contracted out pension scheme members; and

- Third tier – additional voluntary contributions (see glossary) and some personal pensions held in addition to second tier provision.

Individuals who are self-employed are not eligible to join S2P (or formerly SERPS); their second tier pension provision is generally restricted to personal or stakeholder pensions, making any additional provision through non-pension saving. However, there are a wider range of options available to employees and the remainder of this section considers the trends in numbers of employees covered by differing forms of 'second tier pension provision'.

In 1978/79, 13.4 million men out of a total 13.9 million in employment had some form of second tier pension provision, 7.6 million of whom were members of contracted out salary related pension schemes and another 5.8 million were members of SERPS (Figure 6.4). A further 0.5 million male employees had no second tier provision, and their earnings would have been below the NI contributions requirement. During the early 1980s, numbers in contracted out salary related pensions declined and by 1986/87 there were 6.4 million members.

The introduction of personal pensions in 1988 had a major impact on the number of men in SERPS as individuals switched from SERPS to contracted out personal pensions (also called appropriate personal pensions or APPs). In 1987/88 there were a total of 12.1 million men with second tier pension provision: 6.2 million of these were in contracted out salary related schemes, 3.8 million were in SERPS and 1.9 million were in APPs. The number of men with APPs increased over the next five years and in 1992/93 there were 11.2 million men with

Figure **6.4**

Number of employees: by principal type of second tier pension provision[1]

United Kingdom

Millions

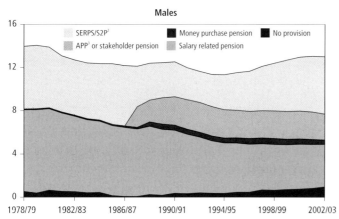

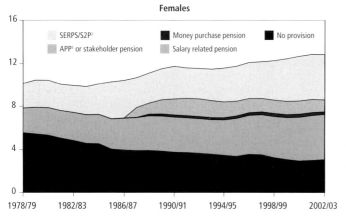

1 Figures for 2001/02 and 2002/03 should be regarded as provisional and may be subject to changes in future releases.
2 State earnings-related pension scheme/state second pension. Those building up provision both in SERPS/S2P and in another type of pension during the course of a year are included under the other type of pension.
3 Appropriate personal pensions.

Source: Department for Work and Pensions

second tier pension provision: 5.2 million of these were in contracted out salary related pension schemes, 2.9 million were in SERPS and 2.8 million had contracted out APPs.

Over the decade since 1992/93 there has been a steady shift to SERPS/S2P provision, most of the decline being in contracted out salary related scheme memberships. In 2002/03 there were 12.1 million men in employment with second tier pension provision, 3.9 million of these were in contracted out salary related pension schemes, 5.3 million were in S2P and 2.4 million had contracted out APPs. One of the factors driving this change has been employers moving away from contracted out salary related occupational pension schemes and setting up contracted in money purchase pension schemes. An additional 1.4 million men not in employment were covered by S2P in

2002/03 following the introduction of S2P qualification through inability to work.

The most marked trend in pension provision for female employees has been the reduction in the number of female employees with no provision, a group that includes both those with earnings below the NI contributions requirement and married women paying reduced rate contributions. The main reasons for this reduction, from 5.6 million females in 1978/79 to 3.1 million in 2002/03 were the removal of the reduced rate option for married women in 1978, coupled with increasing participation in the labour market. The general trends for women in employment are therefore different from those for men and the numbers of women in all forms of second tier pension provision have risen over the period 1978/79 to 2002/03.

The number of female members of contracted out salary related schemes rose from 2.3 million in 1978/79 to 4.2 million in 2002/03, and the number of female employees in the additional state scheme also increased from 2.3 million SERPS members to 4.2 million S2P members over the same period. An additional 2.7 million women not in employment were covered by S2P in 2002/03 following the introduction of S2P qualification through inability to work. Fewer women than men have contracted out APPs, and the number of female employees with this form of provision has shown a decline over the last 10 years, from a peak of 1.6 million in 1992/93 to 1.1 million in 2002/03.

Sources and further reading

Department for Work and Pensions; *Contributions and Qualifying Years 1978/79 to 2002/03.*

Department for Work and Pensions, *Second Tier Pension Provision 1978/79 to 2002/03.*

Private pension scheme membership

- There were an estimated 9.8 million active members of occupational pension schemes in 2004 compared with peak membership of 12.2 million in 1967.

- The proportion of the working-age male population contributing to any private pension fell from 52 per cent to 48 per cent between 1999/2000 and 2003/04. For women, the proportion showed a marginal increase from 39 per cent to 40 per cent.

- In Great Britain in 2003/04, 55 per cent of male employees and 56 per cent of female employees working full time, and 33 per cent of women working part time, were members of their current employer's pension scheme.

- The proportion of self-employed men contributing to a personal pension scheme decreased from 64 per cent in 1998/99 to 49 per cent in 2003/04.

- In 2003/04, 88 per cent of men and 90 per cent of women reporting gross weekly earnings over £600 a week held any private pension, compared with 21 per cent of men and 31 per cent of women earning between £100 and £200 a week.

- In 2003/04 in Great Britain, 72 per cent of both men and women working full time who had been with their current employer for five or more years were members of an occupational pension scheme.

Chapter 7

This chapter discusses membership of all types of non-state pension schemes, referred to here as private pensions. This includes occupational schemes for both private sector and public sector employees, and personal pensions, including stakeholder pensions. The chapter focuses on 'active' members – those belonging to schemes that are currently receiving contributions or building up entitlement. It starts by describing trends in the numbers of people who are members of private pension schemes, looking first at the overall working-age population, then employees and the self-employed. The later sections look at the characteristics of members in 2003/04, length of time with their current employer and the duration of their pension scheme membership.

An individual may be an active member of a number of different pension schemes simultaneously. Employees may be members of an occupational scheme run by their employer or may have an employer-sponsored personal pension. They may also have a personal pension that they have taken out independently, as may non-employees. In addition individuals may be deferred members of a scheme, retaining pension rights with a previous employer, or holding personal pensions that no longer receive contributions. Because of this diversity of provision, there is no single data source that provides reliable estimates of the total number of individuals with some form of pension provision.

HM Revenue and Customs estimated that in broad terms there were 15½ million active members of private pension schemes in 2004 – 10 million whose main form of non-state provision was through an occupational pension scheme, 5 million through a personal or stakeholder pension with an individual or employer contribution, and 0.5 million through a retirement annuity contract (the predecessor to a personal pension).¹ Some people will have more than one form of provision but are counted only once in these estimates.

The various data sources used in this chapter have different coverage and characteristics. For instance, the Family Resources Survey and the General Household Survey are the sources providing the richest information on the characteristics of individuals who are active members of pension schemes. Analyses by the type of scheme they belong to are less reliable because individuals, particularly employees in an employer-sponsored scheme, may not fully understand differences between types of scheme, and may not even be aware that they are a member. The analyses here use the source that is most appropriate for the topic, but this inevitably means that there are differences in the types of pension covered and in the population base between one analysis and another.

Trends

The longest consistent series is of membership of occupational pension schemes in the United Kingdom, figures for which are available since the 1950s from the surveys carried out in selected years by the Government Actuary's Department.

Figure **7.1**

Active members of occupational pension schemes: by sector¹

United Kingdom

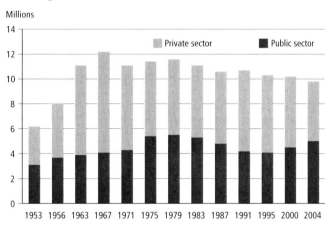

Millions

1 The 2004 split between private and public sectors is not perfectly comparable with splits in earlier years, since from 2000 onwards the public sector figures have included only those members who are in public service schemes. It follows that, from 2000 onwards, figures for the private sector also include members in the wider public sector (such as the Post Office and the BBC).

Source: Occupational Pensions Schemes Survey 2004, *Government Actuary's Department*

There was a marked increase in the number of active members between 1953 and 1967 (from 6.2 million to 12.2 million active members) that has been followed by a steady decline (Figure 7.1). In 2004 there were an estimated 9.8 million active members of occupational pension schemes, 5.0 million in the public sector and 4.8 million in the private sector.

In addition to these active members there were 9.3 million deferred entitlements (see Glossary) to occupational pensions in 2004. These are rights held by people who are no longer actively contributing to schemes, because they have changed employer, for example. This does not represent the number of people with deferred pension rights as an individual may have a deferred entitlement in more than one scheme, and may also be an active member of another scheme.

Estimates of private pension scheme membership from the 2003/04 Family Resources Survey may understate members where the only contribution comes from the National Insurance rebate (see Glossary). Based on figures from this

Figure **7.2**

Working-age[1] membership of a private[2] pension scheme: by sex and pension type

Great Britain

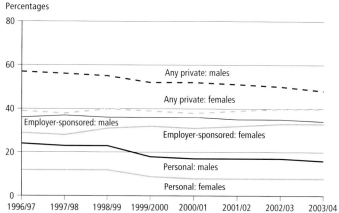

1 Males aged 20 to 64, females aged 20 to 59.
2 Employer-sponsored or personal pension. Data from 1999/2000 onwards are not comparable with earlier data because of the implementation of improvements in government surveys relating to pensions from that date.

Source: Family Resources Survey, Department for Work and Pensions

source, it is estimated that 14.3 million people of working age (between 20 and state pension age) in Great Britain were members in 2003/04, representing 44 per cent of the total 32.5 million working-age population. The proportion of working-age men was slightly higher than that for women, 48 per cent compared with 40 per cent (Figure 7.2). It should be noted that estimates for the years up to and including 1998/99 in Figure 7.2 are not comparable with later years as they include some deferred pension memberships.

There were slightly different trends for men and women. There was a 4 percentage point fall (from 52 to 48 per cent) between 1999/2000 and 2003/04 in the proportion of men contributing to any private pension, or a reduction from 8.5 to 8.0 million individuals. However the proportion of women showed a marginal increase from 39 per cent to 40 per cent over the same period, representing an increase of 0.19 million to 6.25 million individuals.

Membership by employment status

Looking first at employees, the General Household Survey provides the most consistent data source for pension scheme membership over time. In spring 2005 there were 24.7 million employees in employment in the United Kingdom: 11.4 million full-time and 1.2 million part-time men; 7.0 million full-time and 5.1 million part-time women. Participation in employer pension schemes – occupational or employer-sponsored personal pensions – differs for men and women, and for those

working full time and part time. Full-time employees are more likely to be a member of their employer's pension scheme than part-time employees (Figure 7.3).

Figure **7.3**

Employee membership[1] of current employer's pension scheme:[2] by sex

Great Britain

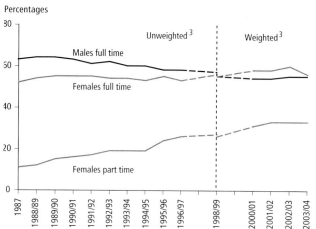

1 Employees aged 16 and over but excluding Youth Trainees and Employment Trainees.
2 Figures for 1997/98 and 1999/2000 have been interpolated as no surveys were carried out in these years.
3 From 1998/99 data are weighted to compensate for non-response and to match known population distributions.

Source: General Household Survey, Office for National Statistics

Almost two thirds (63 per cent) of male employees in Great Britain in 1987 working full time were members of their current employer's pension scheme, this figure falling to 55 per cent in 2003/04. The corresponding proportions for female employees working full time showed a different pattern; 52 per cent were members in 1987, this figure rising to 60 per cent in 2002/03 before falling back to 56 per cent in 2003/04. Among women working part time, there was a sharp increase over the same period, from 11 per cent in 1987 to 33 per cent in 2003/04. This can largely be explained by changes following a European Court of Justice ruling in May 1995 that made it illegal for pension schemes to exclude part-time workers.

Data from the Annual Survey of Hours and Earnings (ASHE) are available only for more recent years, but provide a more reliable indication of the type of scheme that the employee belongs to. Between 1998 and 2004 there was little overall change in the percentage of employees who were members of employer-sponsored pension schemes (Figure 7.4). A fall in the percentage with salary-related private pension schemes (from 45 per cent to 42 per cent) and money purchase schemes (from 9 per cent to 8 per cent) was offset by an

Figure **7.4**

Employee membership of an employer-sponsored[1] pension scheme: by pension type

United Kingdom

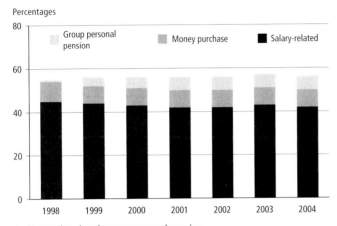

1 Occupational and group personal pension.

Source: Annual Survey of Hours and Earnings, Office for National Statistics

increase in the percentage with group personal pensions (from 1 per cent to 6 per cent). Two per cent of those with one of these forms of provision also had a stakeholder pension. Analysis of the ASHE data for 2004 indicates that an additional 2 per cent of employees not included above have provision through an employer-sponsored stakeholder pension alone.

Figure 7.5 breaks down employees with employer-sponsored pensions between those who are contracted in and contracted out of the state second pension (S2P, formerly state earnings-

Figure **7.5**

Employee membership of an employer-sponsored[1] pension scheme: by whether contracted out or not

United Kingdom

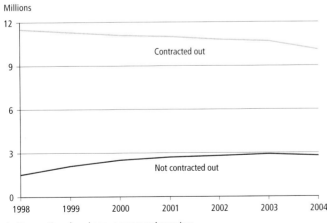

1 Occupational and group personal pension.

Source: Annual Survey of Hours and Earnings, Office for National Statistics

related pension scheme SERPS, see Glossary). In 1998, 11.5 million employees with pensions were contracted out, but by 2004 this figure had fallen to 10.1 million. This decrease was largely confined to male employees. The number of male employees with pensions who were contracted out fell from 6.1 million in 1998 to 4.9 million in 2004. Corresponding figures for female employees with pensions were 5.4 million in 1998 and 5.2 million in 2004.

Turning to the self-employed, 3.6 million workers were self-employed in spring 2005 in the United Kingdom, most (2.3 million) being men working full time. The General Household Survey provides the most consistent information on trends in pension scheme membership for the self-employed. Almost two thirds (66 per cent) of self-employed men working full time in Great Britain belonged to a personal pension scheme in 1991/92, a figure that remained broadly the same until 1998/99. However, between 1998/99 and 2003/04, the proportion fell sharply, from 64 per cent to 49 per cent (Figure 7.6). The proportion of self-employed men who no longer had a personal pension scheme increased from 7 per cent in 1991/92 to 15 per cent in 2003/04, while those who had never had a personal pension scheme rose from 27 per cent to 36 per cent.

Personal pensions were first introduced in 1988, and stakeholder pensions in April 2001. These are the only form of pension that the self-employed can now take out, though some self-employed people will still be investing in a retirement annuity contract set up before 1988. Unlike

Figure **7.6**

Self-employed males:[1] by whether belonging to a personal pension scheme

Great Britain

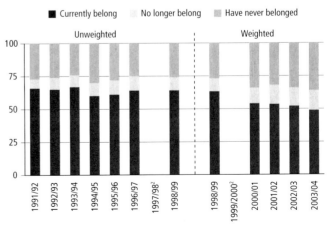

1 Full-time workers only.
2 No surveys were carried out in these years.

Source: General Household Survey, Office for National Statistics

retirement annuity contracts, personal and stakeholder pensions can also be taken out by some employees, and stakeholder pensions can be bought by people who are not in work.

Since the introduction of stakeholder pensions, HM Revenue and Customs has been receiving administrative data (see Glossary) from pension providers, which can be analysed to show the number of individuals with contributions to either a personal or stakeholder pension in the tax year. The data can be broken down by income and employment status, by sex and age, and by region. The figures include pensions where the only contribution was the National Insurance rebate and are therefore larger than the estimated 5 million individuals who contributed themselves or received an employer contribution.

In 2003/04, there were 5.4 million individuals with contributions to personal pensions and 1.4 million to stakeholder pensions. In total 6.5 million individuals had contributions to either a personal or stakeholder pension or to both. The overall numbers were little changed from 2001/02 but there was a small fall in the number of personal pensions offset by an increase in those contributing to stakeholder pensions.

Of the 6.5 million individuals with contributions in 2003/04, some 4.3 million were male and 2.2 million were female. By employment status, 5.2 million were employees and over 1.1 million were self-employed. The remaining very small numbers were not in employment.

Characteristics of pension scheme members in 2003/04

Looking at the proportions of working-age individuals who were members of a private pension scheme in Great Britain in 2003/04 (Figure 7.7), men and women in their 40s were the most likely to be contributing to any private pension. In the 45 to 49 age band, 62 per cent (1.2 million) of men and 47 per cent of women (0.9 million) were active members, as were 61 per cent of men and 46 per cent of women aged 40 to 44. Individuals aged 20 to 24, towards the start of their working lives, were least likely to be contributing (14 per cent of men and 17 per cent of women), but this was the only age band where the proportion of women contributing was higher than for men.

A major reason for the generally higher male membership of pension schemes is the different employment patterns for men and women. Women are less likely to be employed, as discussed in chapter 3. If employed, they are more likely than men to work part time, to have shorter durations of employment, and to have lower incomes; all factors that are associated with lower pension scheme membership.

Differences between the sexes include both an age effect and a cohort effect. For example, the proportion of women of childbearing age with a private pension might always be lower than that of men of the same age as they are less likely to be in employment; but the difference between the sexes for the older age groups also reflects the employment experience of that cohort. When younger cohorts reach the same age, the position might be different.

Figure 7.7

Working-age[1] membership of a private pension scheme:[2] by sex and age, 2003/04

Great Britain

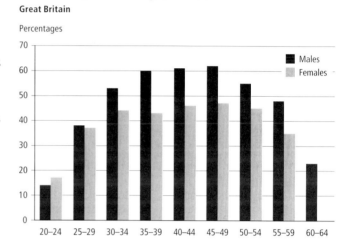

Percentages

1 Males aged 20 to 64, females aged 20 to 59.
2 Employer-sponsored or personal pension.

Source: Family Resources Survey, Department for Work and Pensions

There is a wide variation in the proportion of the population employed in different industry groups who have a private pension (Figure 7.8). In Great Britain in 2003/04 men working in the education sector were the most likely to be members (71 per cent), closely followed by those working in the health and social work sector (69 per cent), and banking and finance (also 69 per cent). In contrast only 21 per cent of male workers in the hotel and catering industry were members of a private pension scheme. For female workers, the highest proportions with a private pension were those working in the banking and finance industry (70 per cent) and education (66 per cent). The lowest proportion was again in the hotel and catering industry (19 per cent).

The wide variation between industry sectors reflects differences in the extent to which employers offer provision (see chapter 11) as well as the rate at which employees take up the provision offered. Some of the sectors with high membership, such as education, and health and social work, are predominantly public sector. A further factor is the balance between employment and self-employment. For instance, in

Figure **7.8**

All employed[1] membership of a private pension scheme:[2] by sex and industry, 2003/04

Great Britain

Percentages

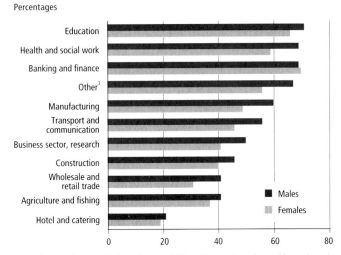

1 Males aged 20 to 64, females aged 20 to 59; employed or self-employed.
2 Employer-sponsored or personal pension.
3 Includes mining and quarrying; electricity, gas and water supply; public administration and defence; and other social and personal services.

Source: Family Resources Survey, Department for Work and Pensions

Figure **7.9**

Full-time employee membership of a private pension scheme: by sex and usual gross weekly earnings,[1] 2003/04

Great Britain

Percentages

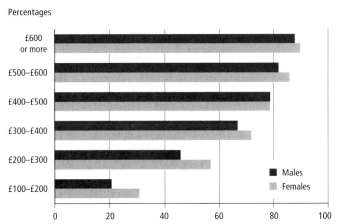

1 Figures for earnings below £100 a week are excluded as sample sizes are too small.

Source: General Household Survey, Office for National Statistics

one of the sectors with a low proportion of membership, agriculture and fishing, there is traditionally a high degree of self-employment, and for most of the 41 per cent of men who were members, the provision was in the form of a personal pension.

The higher people's incomes, the more likely they are to be contributing to a private pension, as Figure 7.9 illustrates for full-time workers. Half of the male employees included in the General Household Survey and covered by this analysis reported weekly earnings less than £287, and half of female employees less than £165. The General Household Survey, though giving the most complete picture of pension scheme membership, is not the primary source for earnings data. These figures differ from other official published earnings figures because of different coverage and sampling.

In 2003/04, 88 per cent of men and 90 per cent of women reporting gross weekly earnings over £600 held any private pension, compared with 21 per cent of men and 31 per cent of women earning between £100 and £200 a week (data for those earning under £100 is based on a small sample and is less reliable). In all earnings ranges, the proportion of women working full time with a private pension was greater than or equal to that for men, the difference being most marked in the lower earnings bands.

Length of time with current employer

The longer employees have worked for their current employer, the more likely they are to be members of either an employer-sponsored or personal pension scheme. The majority of occupational pension schemes have no restriction on eligibility in respect of the employee's length of service with that employer. In the minority of schemes that do operate such a restriction, typical employment requirements are six months, one year or two years. Estimates from the Occupational Pension Schemes Survey 2004 show that, of the 2.76 million active members of open private sector schemes with 12 or more members, 0.25 million active members were in a scheme requiring a minimum employment of more than one year, and a further 0.14 million were in schemes requiring employment of up to one year.

In 2003/04 in Great Britain, 72 per cent of both men and women working full time who had been with their current employer for five or more years were members of an occupational pension scheme (Figure 7.10). Of those who had been with their current employer for less than two years, slightly more women than men were members (34 per cent compared with 28 per cent). For women working part time, 50 per cent of those who had been with their current employer for five or more years were members compared with 16 per cent of those working for an employer for less than two years.

Figure **7.10**

Employee membership of an occupational pension scheme: by sex and length of time with current employer, 2003/04

Great Britain

Percentages

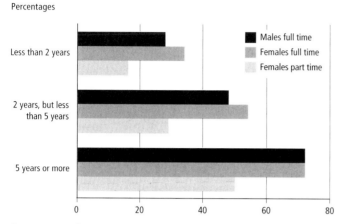

Source: General Household Survey, Office for National Statistics

Looking at employees with personal pensions, the range of take up over length of time with current employer varies less than that for occupational pensions. However, since individuals can continue contributing to a personal pension scheme after they change employer, the length of time with their current employer may understate the length of time they have held the personal pension. In 2003/04, 18 per cent of men in full-time employment with their current employer for less than two years had personal pensions. This figure rose to 25 per cent of those who had been working with their current employer for five or more years (Figure 7.11). For

Figure **7.11**

Employee membership of a personal pension scheme: by sex and length of time with current employer, 2003/04

Great Britain

Percentages

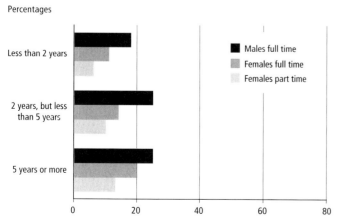

Source: General Household Survey, Office for National Statistics

women working full time, the equivalent percentages ranged from 11 per cent to 20 per cent. Fewer women working part time had personal pensions, irrespective of the length of time with their current employer.

As with employees, the self-employed were more likely to be members of a personal pension scheme the longer they had been in self-employment (Figure 7.12). Figures are averaged over a three-year period because the sample sizes are small. Only 24 per cent of men in Great Britain in 2001/02–2003/04 working full time who had been self-employed for less than two years were members of a personal pension scheme, compared with 60 per cent of those in self-employment for five years or more. The pattern was similar for women in self-employment though their membership was lower overall, particularly for part-timers. Among women working part time who had been self-employed for less than two years, 11 per cent were members, increasing to 35 per cent of those who had been in self-employment for five years or more.

Figure **7.12**

Self-employed membership of a personal pension scheme: by sex and length of time in self-employment, 2001/02–2003/04[1]

Great Britain

Percentages

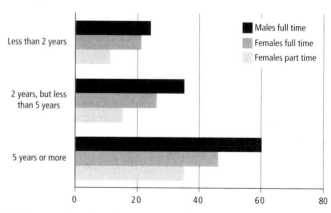

1 *Figures are based on the average over three years as the sample size is small.*

Source: General Household Survey, Office for National Statistics

Duration of membership

Pension benefits generally increase with the length of membership in a scheme, though the exact arrangements will depend on the type of scheme. Estimates from the Family Resources Survey show the length of membership in their current pension scheme for male and female employees in Great Britain in 2001/02–2003/04. A greater proportion of men (46 per cent) than women (36 per cent) in an employer's pension scheme had been members for ten years or more

Figure **7.13**

Employee membership of an employer-sponsored pension scheme: by sex and length of time in scheme, 2001/02–2003/04[1]

Great Britain

Percentages

1 Figures are based on the average over three years as the sample size is small.

Source: Family Resources Survey, Department for Work and Pensions

(Figure 7.13). The difference is most marked for the proportion who had been members over 20 years – 20 per cent of men and 12 per cent of women.

The differences between the sexes are larger for the older age bands, suggesting they are attributable to women experiencing a mid-career break in employment; 44 per cent of men aged 50 to 54 had been pension scheme members for 20 or more years, compared with 23 per cent of women in the same age band.

References

1 Estimate by HM Revenue and Customs for 'Simplifying the Taxation of Pensions: Regulatory Impact Assessment' 2004. Available on the web at: www.hmrc.gov.uk/ria/simplifying-pensions.pdf.

Sources and further reading

Department for Work and Pensions, Family Resources Survey.

Government Actuary's Department (2005) *Occupational pension schemes 2004*. Report of the 12th occupational pensions schemes survey. Available on the web at: www.gad.gov.uk/Publications/docs/Final%20Report%2016Jun2005.pdf.

HM Revenue and Customs website www.hmrc.gov.uk/stats/pensions/menu.

Office for National Statistics, Annual Survey of Hours and Earnings.

Office for National Statistics, General Household Survey.

Pension contributions

- The average employee contribution rate for private sector occupational schemes in 2004 was 4.3 per cent of salary for defined benefit schemes compared with 2.9 per cent for defined contribution schemes.

- 48 per cent of members of defined contribution occupational schemes contributed between 3 and under 4 per cent of their salaries.

- 49 per cent of members in defined benefit occupational schemes contributed at least 6 per cent of their salary.

- The average employer contribution rate to private sector occupational schemes in 2004 was 14.5 per cent of salary for defined benefit schemes compared with 6.0 per cent for defined contribution schemes.

- 94 per cent of employers that ran a group personal pension scheme in 2003 made contributions to the scheme. Just under half of employers offering access to stakeholder pensions did so.

- Total contributions to all types of occupational and personal scheme increased from £37 billion in 1996 to £69 billion in 2004.

- Employee and individual contributions grew steadily from 1996 to 2004 from £14 billion to £21 billion. The rise in employer contributions was greater, from £22 billion to £48 billion.

This chapter first considers the level of contributions to occupational pension schemes made by scheme members and their employers for the different types of pension schemes. It then looks at contribution levels in personal pension schemes, including group personal pensions and stakeholder pensions, before finally presenting aggregate contributions across all pension types. This chapter includes a discussion of the number of members of private sector occupational pension schemes paying different contribution rates, but overall pension scheme membership is covered in chapter 7.

Contribution levels alone do not provide a measure of pension adequacy. The size of an individual's pension fund at retirement also depends on the investment returns received, or the accrual rates in salary related schemes. And as was seen in chapter 5, the level of pension considered adequate in retirement varies between individuals.

There is considerable variation in the level of contributions between schemes, and in the balance between employer and employee contributions. At one extreme employers bear the whole cost of running the pension scheme; these schemes are called non-contributory as their members pay no contributions. At the other extreme there are pension schemes where the employer makes no contribution and the full cost of pension saving is carried by the individual; generally these are personal pension arrangements.

In general a major part of the costs and risks of a defined benefit pension scheme (for example a salary related scheme) falls to the employer, while with most defined contribution pension arrangements the individual member carries the risk that the value of their accrued pension fund at retirement will

not meet their pension needs, see also chapter 11. The amount of the employer contribution to a funded defined benefit pension scheme can vary and is usually based on actuarial estimates (see Glossary) of the fund required to meet payments of scheme benefits when they fall due.

In the 1990s when the strong equity market led to significant growth in fund values, some employers took contribution holidays to reduce pension fund surpluses. The subsequent stock market decline has meant that some pension schemes are not fully funded and employers may be facing the need for additional or special contributions. Such contributions may be in the form of lump sum payments, in which case they are not included in the following analyses of contribution rates.

Private sector occupational pension schemes: employee contribution rates

Changes in contribution rates over time can be examined by looking at the distribution of members across contribution bands. These analyses exclude schemes with fewer than 12 members, which account for a very small proportion of total membership, as data on their contribution rates is not so robust. Some of the changes were in the composition of types of scheme, such as the shift from defined benefit to defined contribution schemes. Overall the number of active members of private sector occupational pension schemes fell from 6.1 million in 1979 to 5.8 million in 1983 and 1987, increased to a peak of 6.5 million in 1991, and then fell to 4.5 million in 2004 (Table 8.1).

The increase in membership of private sector occupational pension schemes in the early 1990s was concentrated in those

Table **8.1**

Active members of private sector occupational pension schemes:[1] by employee contribution rates

United Kingdom   Millions

	1979	1983	1987	1991	1995	2000	2004
Percentage of salary							
Under 3%	0.5	0.4	0.4	0.6	0.8	0.5	0.4
3% to under 5%	1.0	1.1	1.0	1.3	1.6	1.0	0.9
5% to under 6%	2.2	1.8	1.8	1.9	1.9	1.7	0.9
6% and over	0.9	1.3	1.4	1.3	0.8	1.1	1.4
Non-contributory or other[2] basis	1.5	1.2	1.2	1.4	1.1	0.8	0.9
Total[3]	**6.1**	**5.8**	**5.8**	**6.5**	**6.2**	**5.1**	**4.5**

1 *Schemes with 12 or more members only.*
2 *Contributions not as a percentage of earnings.*
3 *Excludes non-respondents.*

Source: **Occupational Pension Schemes Survey 2004,** *Government Actuary's Department*

paying lower contribution rates. The number of members in a non-contributory scheme increased slightly from 1.2 million in 1987 to 1.4 million in 1991, the number of members paying contribution rates of 3 per cent to 5 per cent of salary increased from 1.0 million to 1.3 million over the same period, while the number of members paying higher contribution rates remained much the same. In the mid 1990s the strong equity market meant that many pension schemes were funded more than was permissible under taxation rules. Some employers took contribution holidays, other schemes reduced contribution rates for members, and the number of active members paying contribution rates of 6 per cent or more of their salary fell from 1.3 million in 1991 to 0.8 million in 1995, a change that was matched by an increase in the number of members paying less than 5 per cent of their salary.

The decline in membership between 1995 and 2000 was greatest for those paying lower contribution rates. The number of members paying less than 6 per cent of salary decreased by 1.1 million, and the number in non-contributory schemes fell by 0.3 million, whereas those paying contribution rates of 6 per cent or more increased by 0.3 million. This pattern suggests that some occupational schemes increased contribution rates for employees while others were closed, probably in response to funding deficits. By 2004 total membership had declined to 4.5 million, with the largest decline from 2000 levels (0.8 million) in the group paying contribution rates of 5 per cent to 6 per cent of their salary, a fall partially offset by an increase of 0.3 million in the number of members paying contribution rates of 6 per cent or more.

In 2004, 3.6 million of the 4.6 million active members of private sector occupational pension schemes were in defined benefit schemes and 1.0 million were in defined contribution schemes. The weighted average employee contribution rate for all private sector schemes with 12 or more members was 4.0 per cent of salary. Average employee contributions are generally higher in private sector defined benefit occupational pension schemes than in defined contribution schemes, with a weighted average employee contribution rate of 4.3 per cent of salary compared with 2.9 per cent. These averages include non-contributory schemes.

In schemes where members contribute there was a greater variation in contribution levels across defined benefit schemes than for defined contribution schemes (Figure 8.2). Almost half (48 per cent) of members of defined contribution schemes contributed between 3 and under 4 per cent of their salaries. Around the same proportion (49 per cent) of members in defined benefit schemes were making contributions of at least 6 per cent of their salary, compared with only 9 per cent of members of defined contribution schemes. While 8 per cent of members of defined benefit schemes were making contributions of less than 3 per cent of their salary, 19 per cent of members of defined contribution schemes were doing so.

Private sector occupational pension schemes: employer contribution rates

Turning to employer contributions, the weighted average contribution rate for all private sector schemes with 12 or more members was 12.6 per cent of salary. These contribution

Figure **8.2**

Active members of private sector occupational pension schemes:[1] by type of scheme and employee contribution rates,[2] 2004

United Kingdom

Percentages

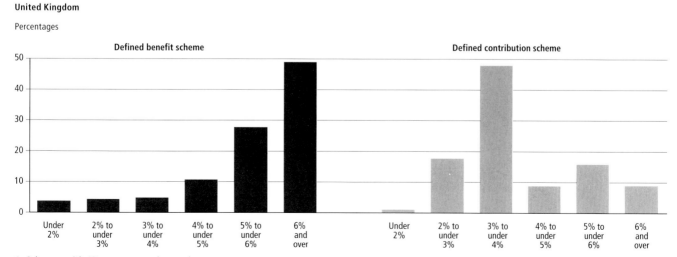

1 Schemes with 12 or more members only.
2 Excludes non-contributory or contributions not as a percentage of earnings, as well as non-responses.

Source: Occupational Pensions Schemes Survey 2004, *Government Actuary's Department*

rates exclude lump sum payments, which can be significant for employers making good deficits in defined benefit schemes. It should also be noted that there is a wide variety of arrangements used for setting employer contributions to defined contribution schemes, and the figures quoted will not include, for example, contributions that are fixed in cash terms rather than based on a percentage of a member's salary.

The general pattern for the distribution of employer contribution rates between different types of scheme is similar to that of employee contributions. The weighted average contribution rate for private sector defined benefit schemes was 14.5 per cent of salary, much higher than the 6.0 per cent for defined contribution schemes. Other things being equal, this will result in higher levels of benefit, though a small part of the difference is attributable to the different characteristics of the schemes and their members:

- Defined contribution schemes are less likely to be contracted out (see Glossary and Table 8.4), and employers contributing to not contracted out schemes pay higher National Insurance contributions that will deliver benefits in the form of additional state pension for their employees (see also chapter 6);

- Employers with defined benefit pension schemes are more likely to offer benefits on ill-health retirement than those with defined contribution schemes. The costs of this would be included within the pension contributions, while other employers may have separate insurance arrangements to cover permanent health insurance.

- Most defined contribution schemes are not as long established as defined benefit schemes. It is too early to assess whether contribution rates will increase as their membership matures.

Sponsoring employers were making contributions of at least 12 per cent of their employees' salary for almost three quarters (72 per cent) of defined benefit scheme members, compared with just 2 per cent of those in defined contribution schemes (Figure 8.3). They were making contributions of under 8 per cent of their employees' salary for 67 per cent of members of defined contribution schemes, compared with just 8 per cent of members of defined benefit schemes.

Table 8.4 illustrates that some, but not a major part, of the difference between employer rates in defined benefit and defined contribution schemes arises from the difference in contracting status. Nearly all defined benefit schemes are contracted out. Around a third of members of defined contribution pension schemes are contracted out, all of whom are in schemes where employer pension contribution levels are less than 12 per cent of their salary, and around half are less than 8 per cent. The other two thirds of those in defined contribution schemes are not contracted out, and the majority of these members are in schemes where employer contribution rates are less than 8 per cent.

Figure **8.3**

Employer contribution rates[1] for active members of private sector occupational pension schemes:[2] by type of scheme, 2004

United Kingdom

Percentages

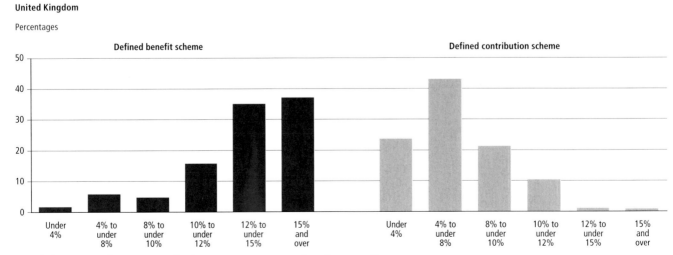

1 Excludes non-contributory or contributions not as a percentage of earnings, as well as non-responses.
2 Schemes with 12 or more members only.

Source: Occupational Pensions Schemes Survey 2004, *Government Actuary's Department*

Table **8.4**

Active members of private sector occupational pension schemes:[1] by employer contribution rate, type of scheme and contracting out status, 2004

United Kingdom

Millions

	Defined benefit scheme		Defined contribution scheme	
	Contracted out	Not contracted out	Contracted out	Not contracted out
Percentage of salary[2]				
Under 8%	0.3	–	0.2	0.4
8% to under 12%	0.5	0.1	0.2	0.1
12% to under 15%	1.1	–	–	–
15% and over	1.2	–	–	–
Total	**3.1**	**0.1**	**0.3**	**0.6**
Non-contributory or other[3] basis	0.1	–	–	–
Non-respondents	0.2	–	–	–
Total	**3.4**	**0.2**	**0.3**	**0.7**

1 Schemes with 12 or more members only.
2 Excludes schemes where contributions were not made by reference to a percentage of the member's salary.
3 Contributions not as a percentage of earnings.

Source: Occupational Pension Schemes Survey 2004, *Government Actuary's Department*

Public sector occupational pension schemes

All public sector occupational pension schemes are defined benefit schemes. Employee contribution rates for the very large schemes, which account for the bulk of public sector membership, are shown in Table 8.5. Membership numbers are covered in chapter 7. The schemes for National Health Service staff, teachers, police officers, firefighters, civil servants and the armed forces are run on an unfunded, pay-as-you-go basis. Employer contributions are largely an internal accounting transaction within government. These 'imputed' or 'notional' contributions are calculated to represent the amounts that would be required to meet the accruing liabilities of the schemes if they were funded.

All local authorities run funded pension schemes; the funds are held by individual authorities or small groups of authorities, but employee contribution rates are common across all authorities. The employer contributions to these funded local authority schemes are determined, in a similar way to those for private sector occupational pension schemes, by means of regular actuarial reviews (see Glossary).

Table **8.5**

Employee contribution rates[1] for public sector occupational pension schemes

United Kingdom

Percentages

Armed forces	Non-contributory
Civil service	3.5/1.5[2]
Firefighters	11
Local government	6[3]
National Health Service staff	6[3]
Police officers	11
Teachers	6

1 Value of pension is wholly or partly taken into account in the assessment of pay levels.
2 3.5 per cent is the rate for new members. A large closed group contributes at 1.5 per cent.
3 Small closed groups contribute at 5 per cent.

Source: Occupational Pension Schemes Survey 2004, *Government Actuary's Department*

Employer-sponsored personal pensions: contribution rates

Instead of an occupational scheme, some employers operate a group personal pension scheme for their employees. The employees are individual members of the personal pension scheme, but the administration costs may be lower than they would be if the employee arranged a personal pension independently.

Employers may also provide access to an employer-sponsored stakeholder pension, either in addition to an occupational pension scheme or as the main form of pension provision. Employers that run an occupational or employer-sponsored pension scheme may also set up arrangements with individual employees to make contributions to the employee's personal pension scheme.

Whereas contributions to defined contribution occupational pension schemes are generally made on the basis of a percentage of salary, contributions to personal pension schemes are sometimes a fixed amount of money per employee. Table 8.6 shows information on the level of employer contributions as either a percentage of salary or as a fixed amount, as appropriate.

Less than half of employers offering access to stakeholder pensions made a contribution to the pension scheme. Where employers made a contribution, more employers made contributions based on a fixed percentage of salary than as an amount of money. The majority of small employers offering a stakeholder pension were making contributions of 3 to 4 per cent of salary, while those making contributions on the basis of a fixed amount of money were most likely to contribute £5 per week or less.

Table **8.6**

Employer contributions[1] to group personal pensions, employer-sponsored stakeholder pensions and employee personal pensions: by size of organisation, 2003

Great Britain   Percentages

	Group personal pensions		Stakeholder pensions		Employee personal pensions	
	Number of employees[2]		Number of employees[2]		Number of employees[2]	
	1 to 19	20 and over	5 to 19	20 and over	1 to 19	20 and over
No contribution	*6*	*6*	*55*	*51*	*..*	*..*
Percentage of pay	*58*	*84*	*30*	*39*	*56*	*76*
of which:						
Less than 3%	*7*	*6*	*0*	*6*	*20*	*16*
3% to 3.9%	*9*	*22*	*17*	*10*	*-*	*6*
4% to 4.9%	*3*	*11*	*0*	*2*	*-*	*8*
5% to 5.9%	*6*	*25*	*6*	*13*	*11*	*17*
6% to 10%	*22*	*17*	*6*	*7*	*12*	*24*
More than 10%	*11*	*4*	*0*	*2*	*12*	*5*
Percentage paying a fixed amount	*35*	*10*	*15*	*9*	*44*	*24*
of which:						
Up to £5 per week	*6*	*1*	*6*	*3*	*5*	*-*
£5.01 to £10 per week	*3*	*1*	*4*	*1*	*4*	*2*
£10.01 to £15 per week	*1*	*1*	*3*	*1*	*6*	*-*
£15.01 to £25 per week	*1*	*0*	*1*	*2*	*17*	*5*
£25.01 to £50 per week	*22*	*2*	*2*	*1*	*8*	*4*
More than £50 per week	*3*	*4*	*0*	*1*	*4*	*12*
All employers responding	*100*	*100*	*100*	*100*	*100*	*100*

1 For group personal pensions and employee personal pensions average contribution over the last three years; for stakeholder pensions average since the scheme was set up in 2001/02.
2 Total employees in the company, not those covered by pension provision. However if there were no active members, the scheme is excluded from this analysis.

Source: **Employers' Pension Provision Survey 2003,** *Department for Work and Pensions*

Where employers run a group personal pension scheme, 94 per cent make contributions to these schemes. Larger employers (20 or more employees) are more likely to make contributions based on a fixed percentage of salary (84 per cent) than small employers (58 per cent), and the average level of contributions was much higher than for stakeholder pensions. In 2003, 33 per cent of small employers offering a group personal pension made contributions of 6 per cent of salary or more and 25 per cent made contributions of £25 per week or more. Comparable results for larger employers were 21 per cent making contributions of 6 per cent of salary or more and 6 per cent making contributions of £25 per week or more.

For 83 per cent of employers who set up personal pension arrangements with individual employees, these arrangements had been put in place for only one or two employees. The wide range of contribution levels in Table 8.6 reflects the varied character of these arrangements.

Personal and stakeholder pensions: amounts contributed

Table 8.7 shows the average annual contribution per individual in 2003/04 to personal and stakeholder pensions (both employer-sponsored and other). The average amounts include contributions from all sources.

Average annual contributions to both personal and stakeholder pensions increased with earned income. For employees, the average annual contribution to personal pensions increased from £930 for those earning less than £10,000 to £3,990 for those earning over £30,000. These were higher than contributions to stakeholder pensions, the comparable figures being £790 and £3,320. For the self-employed there was no marked difference between the level of contributions to personal pensions and stakeholders, and the average contribution to either type increased from £1,030 for those earning less than £10,000 to £4,590 for those earning over £30,000.

Average annual contributions for stakeholder pensions were higher for the self-employed than for employees in the same income band, though there was no consistent pattern for personal pensions. The self-employed are more reliant on private pensions as they do not have access to the state second pension system, see chapter 6.

In May 2005, HM Revenue and Customs published new data showing the total level of contributions to all forms of non-occupational pensions since 1990/91 (Figure 8.8). Employer and employee/individual contributions show steady increases in most years. The steady decline in retirement annuities, the predecessor to personal pensions, reflects the fact that no

Table **8.7**

Average annual contributions[1,2] to personal and stakeholder pensions: by status and earned income, 2003/04

United Kingdom   £

	Personal pensions	Stakeholder pensions	Personal and stakeholder pensions
Employees			
Range of earned income (lower limit)			
£0	930	790	920
£10,000	1,240	840	1,220
£20,000	1,890	1,280	1,900
£30,000	3,990	3,320	4,120
All employees	1,880	1,290	1,860
Self-employed			
Range of earned income (lower limit)			
£0	960	1,120	1,030
£10,000	1,190	1,060	1,230
£20,000	1,610	1,510	1,680
£30,000	4,220	5,120	4,590
All self-employed	1,890	1,990	2,000
Other[3]	1,980	2,000	2,020
Total	1,880	1,430	1,890

1 Includes gross individual, employer and minimum contributions.
2 Contributions are based on what has actually been contributed in the year, so the overall average will not be the typical annual average for those who have started making regular contributions part of the way through the year.
3 Other includes children, people in full-time education, carers, and the unemployed.

Source: HM Revenue and Customs

new contracts could be taken out after 1 July 1988. Free-standing additional voluntary contributions (FSAVCs, see Glossary) can be made by members of occupational schemes; the decline since 1999/2000 reflects that many individuals have chosen to save through stakeholder pensions rather than FSAVCs, partly because the administration costs are lower and partly because stakeholders provide a more flexible method of saving. Minimum contributions represent the rebate paid by HM Revenue and Customs to individuals who have used their personal or stakeholder pension to contract out of the state second pension. The formula used to calculate minimum contributions changed in 1993/94 and again in 1998/99. Year on year comparisons may also be affected by changes in the time taken to process payments.

Figure **8.8**

Total personal and stakeholder pensions, retirement annuity contracts (RACs)[1] and free-standing additional voluntary contributions (FSAVCs): by contribution type

United Kingdom

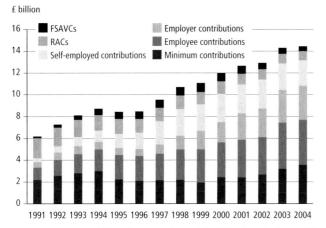

£ billion

Legend:
- FSAVCs
- RACs
- Self-employed contributions
- Employer contributions
- Employee contributions
- Minimum contributions

1991 1992 1993 1994 1995 1996 1997 1998 1999 2000 2001 2002 2003 2004

1 No new RACs could be taken out after 1 July 1998, though those with contracts at this date could continue to contribute to them.

Source: HM Revenue and Customs

Aggregate pension contributions

Total contributions to all types of private pension schemes increased from £37 billion in 1996 to £69 billion in 2004 (Figure 8.9). These include employer contributions, employee/individual contributions, minimum contributions and notional or imputed contributions to unfunded public sector schemes. The figures involve an element of estimation because of the difficulty of identifying 'new' contributions net of double counting that arises because of transfers and investment flows between pension providers. These data issues are discussed in two articles published on the National Statistics website in 2004 and 2005 (see sources and further reading).

Employee and individual contributions have grown steadily from £14 billion in 1996 to £21 billion in 2004. Employer contributions have shown more growth, increasing from £22 billion to £48 billion over the same period. There was a marked increase in the most recent years driven mainly by employer's contributions to funded occupational schemes, which rose from £16 billion in 2001 to £30 billion in 2004.

Table **8.9**

Contributions to private pension schemes

United Kingdom

£ billion

	1996	1997	1998	1999	2000	2001	2002	2003	2004
Funded occupational schemes	**17**	**18**	**20**	**21**	**23**	**23**	**26**	**32**	**37**
of which:									
employers	13	13	14	15	16	16	19	25	30
employees	5	5	6	6	7	7	7	7	7
Unfunded occupational schemes	**10**	**10**	**11**	**11**	**12**	**13**	**15**	**16**	**18**
of which:									
employers	7	7	8	8	9	9	10	11	12
employees	2	3	3	3	3	3	4	5	6
Personal pension schemes	**9**	**10**	**11**	**12**	**13**	**13**	**14**	**14**	**15**
of which:									
employers	2	3	3	4	4	4	5	6	6
employees and individuals	7	8	8	8	9	8	9	9	8
Total contributions to pension schemes	**37**	**39**	**41**	**44**	**47**	**49**	**54**	**63**	**69**
of which:									
employers	22	23	25	27	29	30	35	42	48
employees and individuals	14	16	16	18	18	19	20	20	21

Source: Office for National Statistics

These totals include both normal contributions and 'special' or 'additional' employer contributions; the latter are generally lump sum payments to reduce or remove any deficit between the assets and liabilities of defined benefit schemes. A breakdown of employer contributions between normal and additional is available only for self-administered occupational schemes, as discussed in the section on income of these schemes in chapter 12. Additional contributions to these schemes increased from £2 billion in 2001 to £8 billion in 2004. Increases in normal contributions may also reflect increased payments to reduce deficits as some employers make a single payment that does not distinguish between a 'normal' and 'special' element, while others may have increased their regular contribution rates in response to a deficit.

Sources and further reading

Department for Work and Pensions, *Employers' Pension Provision Survey 2003*.

Government Actuary's Department, *Occupational Pension Scheme Survey 2004 (OPSS 2004)*.

HM Revenue and Customs website: www.hmrc.gov.uk/stats/pensions/menu

National Statistics website: Forrest C, Penneck P and Tily G (2004) Private Pensions Estimates and the National Accounts, *Economic Trends* No. 609, pp 36–46, Office for National Statistics. www.statistics.gov.uk/CCI/article.asp?ID=910

National Statistics website: Penneck P and Tily G (2005) *Private Pension Contributions,* Office for National Statistics www.statistics.gov.uk/CCI/article.asp?ID=1198

Individual pension wealth

- In 2002/03, 55 per cent of men and 73 per cent of women with personal and stakeholder pension funds had a total fund value of less than £10,000.

- There is a broad relationship between the level of earnings and size of personal and stakeholder pension funds. Half of those individuals with pension funds of £50,000 or more earned £30,000 or more in 2001/02.

- Estimates of personal and occupational wealth show a very wide distribution. For men aged 50 to 54 in 2002, the median value was estimated at £75,000.

- The median value of personal and occupational wealth for women aged 50 to 54 is estimated at £6,000, reflecting the fact that many women do not have private pension provision in their own right.

- Median state pension wealth is less widely distributed. Estimates for people aged 50 to 54 in 2002 were £41,000 for men and £54,000 for women.

This chapter looks at the value of pension wealth held by individuals. An individual may have actual pension wealth held in an occupational money purchase pension scheme or in a personal or stakeholder pension fund; or less tangible pension entitlements based on contributions to the state pension scheme or an occupational salary-related pension scheme. Direct estimates of the value of pension fund wealth are available only for personal and stakeholder pensions. The chapter starts by examining the distribution of these fund values and then provides estimates of broader pension wealth derived from survey data.

Personal pension fund values

Since 2001/02, pension providers have been required to report to HM Revenue and Customs the value of funds held for all individuals holding a personal and/or stakeholder pension. This requirement does not extend to other forms of pension saving, so figures do not take account of occupational pensions, retirement annuity contracts (predecessors of personal pensions), or additional voluntary contributions.

There were 9.4 million individuals holding personal and stakeholder pensions in the United Kingdom in 2003, 5.8 million men and 3.6 million women (Figure 9.1). Where an individual has more than one personal or stakeholder pension fund, the analysis shows the aggregate value of all those funds, rather than the values of the separate funds.

Figure **9.1**

Number of individuals holding personal and stakeholder pensions: by sex and fund value,[1] 2002/03

United Kingdom

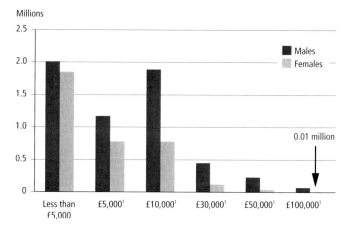

1 Lower limit of fund value.

Source: HM Revenue and Customs

The fund values include rebates from National Insurance for those contracted out (see Glossary) of the earnings-related element of the state pension system. It is not possible to distinguish this compulsory element from the voluntary saving that individuals and/or their employers may also have made.

Table **9.2**

Number of individuals holding personal and stakeholder pensions:[1] by employment status, annual earnings[2] and fund value, 2002/03

United Kingdom

Thousands

	Fund value (lower limit)						
	Less than £5,000	£5,000	£10,000	£30,000	£50,000	£100,000	Total
Earners[3]							
Less than £10,000	1,410	550	570	90	40	10	**2,670**
£10,000–£19,999	1,470	720	890	140	50	10	**3,270**
£20,000–£29,999	590	390	590	130	50	10	**1,760**
£30,000 and over	310	270	600	210	120	50	**1,560**
Total	**3,780**	**1,930**	**2,650**	**570**	**260**	**70**	**9,260**
Non-earners[4]	90	30	10	0	0	0	**140**
Total	**3,870**	**1,960**	**2,660**	**570**	**260**	**80**	**9,400**

1 Individuals holding a personal pension, a stakeholder pension or both.
2 Earned income during 2001/02.
3 Includes employees and the self-employed.
4 Includes those in receipt of a pension, children, those in full-time education, carers, the unemployed and others.

Source: HM Revenue and Customs

The average value of funds in personal and stakeholder pensions held by men was higher than those held by women; 55 per cent of men and 73 per cent of women held funds with a total value of under £10,000, and 87 per cent of men and 95 per cent of women held funds with a total value of under £30,000.

Table 9.2 shows a broad relationship between the level of earnings and size of personal and stakeholder pension funds. Half of those individuals with pension funds of £50,000 or more earned £30,000 or more in 2001/02. A further 15 per cent earned less than £10,000 in the same period and may have accumulated a large pension fund through higher earnings in earlier years. The majority of earners with personal and stakeholder pension funds, (61 per cent) had earnings of less than £20,000 in 2001/02.

The age distribution of individuals with personal and stakeholder pensions is similar for both men and women, with a third of individuals aged 35 to 44, around a quarter

aged 25 to 34 and a further quarter aged 45 to 54 (Figure 9.3). Not surprisingly, older individuals tend to have higher fund values; 22 per cent of men aged 55 and over had funds over £30,000 compared with 12 per cent of men aged 35 to 44. The comparable figures for women were 14 and 4 per cent respectively.

When comparing the distribution of fund values across different age bands, it should be noted that older individuals are more likely to have other personal pension wealth in the form of retirement annuities or additional voluntary contributions. Although existing retirement annuity contracts could be continued, no new ones have been taken out since 1988 when personal pensions were first introduced. A further point that affects comparison is that individuals over 50 may already have taken part of their pension fund as income (known as 'income drawdown') and in these cases the fund value represents the remaining part of their original pension wealth. However, only a relatively small number of people with larger pension funds are in a position to use income drawdown.

The regional distribution of individuals with personal and stakeholder pension funds is broadly similar to that of the general population (Figure 9.4). Overall, 15 per cent of individuals with personal and stakeholder pension funds lived in the South East and 32 per cent with fund values in excess of £30,000 lived in London and in the South East.

Figure **9.3**

Number of individuals holding personal and stakeholder pensions:[1] by sex, age and fund value, 2002/03

United Kingdom

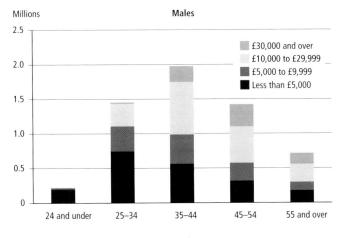

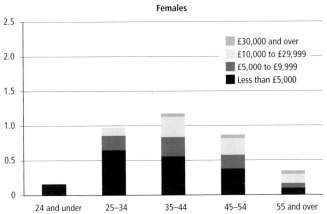

1 Individuals holding a personal pension, a stakeholder pension or both.

Source: HM Revenue and Customs

Figure **9.4**

Number of individuals holding personal and stakeholder pensions:[1] by region[2] and fund value, 2002/03

United Kingdom

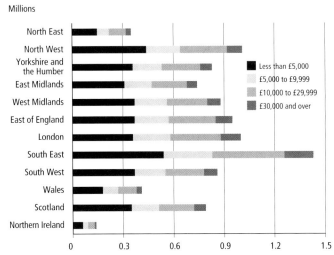

1 Individuals holding a personal pension, a stakeholder pension or both.
2 Figures for England as a whole are: 3.28 million (less than £5,000), 1.67 million (£5,000 to £9,999), 2.30 million (£10,000 to £29,999) and 0.80 million (£30,000 and over), totalling 8.05 million.

Source: HM Revenue and Customs

Looking at the distribution of individuals across the fund bands, there was some tendency for individuals in London and in the South East to have larger fund values. The proportion of individuals with funds of less than £5,000 varied from 45 per cent in Wales to 36 per cent in London, compared with 41 per cent for the United Kingdom as a whole. Similarly, the proportion of individuals with funds of more than £30,000 varied between 12 per cent in London and the South East, and 7 per cent in Northern Ireland, compared with 10 per cent for the United Kingdom as a whole.

Estimated pension wealth

Information on the extent that individuals have built up entitlement to the basic state pension is covered in chapter 6, but these entitlements are not presented as estimates of pension wealth. Similarly, there are no data sources that provide direct estimates of the monetary value of an individual's entitlements built up in occupational pensions. However, the 2002 English Longitudinal Study of Ageing (ELSA) collected detailed information about pensions and pension entitlements

of all types. Using this data, in 2005 the Institute for Fiscal Studies published estimates of the value of individual state pension wealth, and personal and occupational pension wealth.

These estimates have been calculated using a broad range of assumptions about working patterns and economic indicators (see box). They are restricted to individuals aged 50 to state pension age (SPA see Glossary), a group whose retirement pensions will largely be determined by the extent of their existing pension savings as they will have limited opportunities and time to change their savings behaviour before they retire. They are not representative of the population as a whole, and may not be representative of future cohorts reaching the age of 50 who will have experienced different economic and social factors during their earlier life.

Figure 9.5 shows the estimated individual private pension wealth of men and women aged 50 to SPA, including both occupational and personal pensions. It shows both mean and median wealth. As the distribution of wealth is so wide, estimates of the mean wealth are distorted by the small

Pension wealth assumptions

This box provides a brief, simplified summary of the pension wealth calculations used by the Institute for Fiscal Studies (IFS). Full details are presented in IFS Working Paper W05/09 *Estimating pension wealth of ELSA respondents.*

Different assumptions are used for state pension and private pension wealth. In each case, it is assumed that the individual receives their pension at the earliest possible age (their current age for private pensions and state pension age for state pensions) and receives pension income between that age and their average life expectancy (calculated on a sex and age-specific basis). The pension income in all future years is discounted back to 2002 (using a 5 per cent nominal discount rate) to obtain the estimate of pension wealth. The calculations take into account both current pension provision and deferred pension rights in schemes operated by a previous employer.

Personal pension wealth and private pension wealth for money purchase (defined contribution schemes): Using the pension fund values in 2002 as reported in the survey, assume that the individual retires in 2002 and immediately converts their fund to annual income in the form of annuity. It is assumed that the individual receives the same level of annual annuity income between 2002 and their life expectancy. If individuals were unable to provide a pension fund value, an estimated value was

calculated using the information provided by other respondents with similar characteristics.

Private pension wealth for salary related pensions: Information collected from respondents provides details of the length of pensionable service with current and previous employers, the accrual rate and the method of calculating the pension as a proportion of the individual's salary, and the value of a lump sum, where appropriate. If the individual retires before the normal retirement age for their scheme, the value of the pension is reduced by a value known as an actuarial reduction (see Glossary). The most common reduction is 4 per cent for each year between the retirement age and the normal retirement age for the scheme. Taken together, this information provides an estimate of the value of the pension in 2002. It is assumed that the individual receives this pension income between 2002 and their life expectancy, the annual pension being indexed at an inflation rate of 2.5 per cent where appropriate.

State pension wealth: Using information about the individual's most recent employment and whether they are a member of a contracted out pension scheme, it is assumed that the individual receives basic state pension and, where appropriate, additional pension (state earnings-related pension and state second pension), between state pension age and their life expectancy.

proportion of individuals with very high pension wealth. The median, which is the middle point with half the population above and half below, is considerably lower than the mean value for all age groups. These results are consistent with the personal and stakeholder pension fund values in Figure 9.1, which shows a small number of high value funds and a large number of small value funds.

Figure **9.5**

Individual private pension wealth: by sex and age group,[1] 2002

England

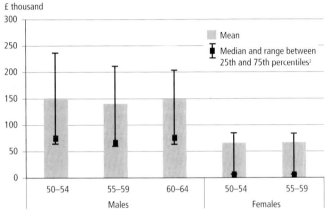

1 Assuming retirement in 2002.
2 See Glossary for an explanation of percentiles.

Source: Estimating pension wealth of ELSA respondents, The Institute for Fiscal Studies Working Papers W05/09

The mean value of individual private pension wealth for men aged 50 to 54 was £151,000 compared with £66,000 for women of the same age. Median private pension wealth estimates for the same age group were £75,000 for men and £6,000 for women. The wide distribution is illustrated by the quartile range (see Glossary). For men aged 50 to 54, the bottom 25 per cent had fund values of £64,000 or less, while the top 25 per cent held fund values of £236,000 or more. The equivalent figures for the bottom 25 per cent of women are zero, reflecting the fact that a large number of women have no private pension provision in their own right, while the top 25 per cent of women held values of £83,000 or more.

There is a marked difference between the average pension fund values for men and women, because many women in these age bands gave up work when they had children, or worked part time. Women are more likely than men to work part time, to be in low paid jobs and to work for small employers that are less likely to provide pension schemes. However, the difference in the value of private pension funds for men and women is exaggerated in the pension wealth estimates presented in Figure 9.5 because the calculation method for the value of a salary-related occupational pension

assigns to one individual in a married couple, the value of any spouse's pension that would be received by their partner after their death. Because women, on average, live longer than men, occupational pension schemes that provide a spouse's pension are more likely to pay a pension to a surviving widow than widower, and the estimated value of the survivor's pension is more likely to be added to the value of the man's pension fund.

Figure 9.6 shows the estimated individual state pension wealth, including additional pension where appropriate, of men and women aged 50 to SPA. The narrowness of the quartile range around the median value shows that the distribution of state pension wealth is less spread out than estimates of private pension wealth shown in Figure 9.5.

Figure **9.6**

Individual state pension wealth: by sex and age group,[1] 2002

England

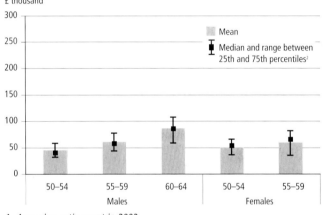

1 Assuming retirement in 2002.
2 See Glossary for an explanation of percentiles.

Source: Estimating pension wealth of ELSA respondents, The Institute for Fiscal Studies Working Papers W05/09

Median values are higher for women than for men in the same age bands, partly reflecting the fact that women in these age groups will reach SPA before men. Also women, on average, live longer than men, so these women will receive their state pension for more years than men, resulting in a higher estimated state pension wealth.

The mean value of individual state pension wealth for all men aged 50 to 54 was £46,000 compared with £51,000 for women of the same age. Median pension wealth estimates for the same group were £41,000 for men and £54,000 for women. However, the differences between the pension wealth values do not reflect the full value of the difference between the sexes, because the calculation method for the value of the earnings-related component of the state pension for an individual uses the practice adopted for the calculation for occupational pensions, and assigns to an individual (usually a man), the value of any spouse's pension that would be received by his partner after his death. Because women, on average, live longer than men, women are more likely to receive this state retirement pension as a surviving widow than men as surviving widowers. Currently survivor pensions are only paid to widows, but from 2009 this entitlement will be extended to widowers who satisfy certain entitlement conditions.

Figure **9.7**

Individual total pension wealth: by sex and age group,[1] 2002

England

£ thousand

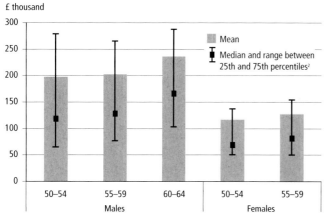

1 Assuming retirement in 2002.
2 See Glossary for an explanation of percentiles.

Source: Estimating pension wealth of ELSA respondents, The Institute for Fiscal Studies Working Papers W05/09

Figure 9.7 shows the estimated total pension wealth for individuals aged 50 to SPA, combining the components illustrated in Figures 9.5 and 9.6. The mean value of total individual pension wealth (state pension wealth plus private pension wealth from personal and occupational pensions) for all men aged 50 to 54 was £198,000 compared with £117,000 for women of the same age. Median total pension wealth estimates for the same group were £119,000 for men and £69,000 for women.

Sources and further reading

Since April 2001, all personal (including stakeholder) pension providers have been obliged to supply Inland Revenue with details of individuals transacting personal pensions business with them. Analyses are available at www.hmrc.gov.uk/stats/pensions/menu.

Banks J, Emmerson C and Tatlow G (2005)
Estimating pension wealth of ELSA respondents,
The Institute for Fiscal Studies, Working Papers W05/09
www.ifs.org.uk/publications.php?publication_id=3369

Non-pension wealth

- 89 per cent of all households in 2003/04 had a current account with a bank or building society, 33 per cent held Individual Savings Accounts and 22 per cent held stocks and shares.

- In 2002, men had greater median net financial wealth than women, an estimated £14,400 compared with £10,500 for all over 50.

- Over three quarters (77 per cent) of all individuals aged 50 and over had net housing wealth greater than zero.

- In 2002, over 93 per cent of all individuals aged 50 and over in England had total non-pension wealth greater than zero. The median figure for all individuals was £126,700.

- People aged between 50 and state pension age in work and contributing to a private pension in 2002 had median total non-pension wealth of £164,000.

- In 2002 people who had never had a private pension scheme had median total non-pension wealth of £104,500 for those in paid work and £36,000 for others.

- Individuals aged 60 to 74 assessed their likelihood of receiving an inheritance of £100,000 or more at under 5 per cent on average.

Chapter 10

Earlier chapters have looked at pension scheme membership and the value of pensions that individuals are building up for retirement. This chapter focuses on other ways that people save or increase their income for retirement. It covers financial assets, housing wealth, total non-pension wealth, and finally expectations of receiving an inheritance, looking at how such assets are distributed and at the demographic characteristics of individuals with different forms of savings. This chapter looks at the distribution of wealth held in various forms and chapter 13 presents figures for the aggregate wealth of the household sector.

When considering the extent to which non-pension wealth might be used to replace or supplement pension wealth, it would be useful to consider how the two are related, but there are no data sources that measure directly both pension and non-pension wealth for all ages. However, some of the following analyses suggest that those who are least likely to be accumulating pension provision for their retirement also tend to have lower holdings of other types of asset.

Ownership of financial assets

Financial assets take many different forms, the most common being a current account with a bank or building society. Figure 10.1 shows the percentage of households with various types of financial account in the United Kingdom in 2003/04. Looking at all households, most (89 per cent) had a current account, 54 per cent had other bank or building society accounts, 33 per cent held Individual Savings Accounts (ISAs), 23 per cent held Premium Bonds and 22 per cent held stocks and shares. Only 6 per cent of households had no financial accounts at all.

Looking only at households with one or more adults over state pension age (see Glossary), the percentages who held accounts of various types were generally similar to those for all households. They were slightly more likely to have ISAs (37 per cent) and Premium Bonds (29 per cent), but slightly less likely to have a current account (85 per cent). Pensioner households were also more likely (8 per cent) to hold National Savings Bonds, including Pensioners Guaranteed Income Bonds or 'granny bonds', than all households (4 per cent). Analyses in the rest of this chapter look at saving and wealth on an individual rather than household basis.

Successive governments have sought to encourage saving through various tax-privileged savings schemes, the most recent being ISAs, which were launched in April 1999 as the successor to Personal Equity Plans (PEPs) and Tax Exempt Special Savings Accounts (TESSAs). Despite their relatively recent introduction, ISAs – which may be a cash or an equity-based investment – have become a commonly held asset.

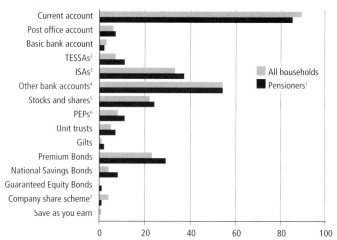

Figure 10.1

Proportion of households with different types of saving, 2003/04

United Kingdom

Percentages

1 Households with one or more adults over state pension age.
2 Tax Exempt Special Savings Accounts.
3 Individual Savings Accounts.
4 Including building societies.
5 Includes membership of a share club.
6 Personal Equity Plans.
7 Including profit sharing.

Source: Family Resources Survey, Department for Work and Pensions

People hold ISAs for a variety of purposes. Unlike savings held in pension form, there are no government restrictions on withdrawing funds from an ISA at any time, so they may be used for either short-term saving or long-term investment. Some people may use them to supplement, or as a substitute for, pension provision.

The most comprehensive information from HM Revenue and Customs administrative data (see Glossary) suggests that around one in three adults hold an ISA, but there is considerable variation between age groups, illustrated in Figure 10.2. This shows the distribution of ownership of ISAs and two other popular types of savings that may be used to supplement pension provision, Premium Bonds and stocks and shares. In 2003/04, ISAs were particularly popular among the retiring or recently retired age groups, with 40 per cent of those aged 60 to 64 holding this type of asset. Stocks and shares were held by 17 per cent of all adults, and Premium Bonds by 16 per cent, with the highest percentage of the latter among those aged 65 to 74 (27 per cent). There was little overall variation between men and women in type of saving, although a slightly higher percentage of men than women (19 per cent compared with 15 per cent) had stocks and shares.

Figure **10.2**

Selected type of saving: by age, 2003/04
United Kingdom

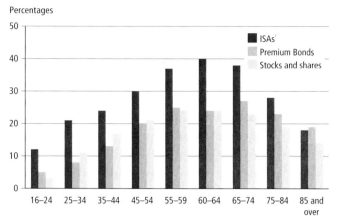

1 Individual Savings Accounts.

Source: Family Resources Survey, Department for Work and Pensions

Figure **10.3**

Average market value of PEP[1] and ISA[2] holdings:[3] by sex and income, 2001/02
United Kingdom

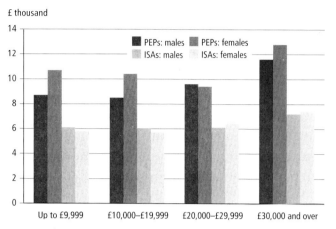

1 Personal Equity Plans.
2 Individual Savings Accounts.
3 For males aged 50 to 64, females aged 50 to 59.

Source: HM Revenue and Customs

Value of ISA and PEP holdings by individuals

Information on the value of assets held by individuals is not generally available, with the exception of ISAs and their predecessor, the PEP. While no subscriptions to PEPs could be made after 5 April 1999, savers with PEPs can continue to hold them under the current rules. Figure 10.3 presents data from HM Revenue and Customs for the average value of holdings for the age groups approaching state pension age, men aged 50 to 64 and women aged 50 to 59, some of whom will already have retired. Individuals can have several PEPS or ISAs and these figures represent the total holdings of each type of asset for an individual, rather than the average of separate holdings.

In 2001/02 (the latest year for which data was available) the average market value of holdings was £10,130 for PEPs and £6,230 for the newer ISAs, which have a lower cap than did PEPs on the amounts that can be invested each year. There is little variation between average holdings for those with income up to £30,000 but average market values are higher for those with incomes above that.

For PEPs, women with income of £30,000 and over a year had the highest average market value, at £12,770. The £20,000 to £29,999 income range was the only one where men had holdings of PEPs with a higher average value than women. For ISAs, women with incomes of £20,000 or more had holdings with slightly higher average market values than men, while the reverse was true for those earning under £20,000 a year. The annual limits on the amounts that can be subscribed may result in a more even distribution between men and women than tends to be the case for other types of savings.

Looking more widely at the value of all types of wealth, the only data source currently available is the English Longitudinal Study of Ageing (ELSA). As the name suggests, this only covers England, and only people aged 50 and over. Although this is the most relevant age group for those approaching and entering into retirement and their associated income needs, it should be borne in mind that future cohorts will not necessarily have had the same working or saving experience so their financial position on reaching the age of 50 may be different.

Net financial wealth

Net financial wealth is savings and investments *minus* debt. This debt does not include outstanding mortgages, which are netted off housing wealth. Financial wealth may include lump sums received from private pension plans, leading to higher wealth among the recently retired than among those who have yet to retire.

As the distribution of wealth is so wide, estimates of the mean wealth would be distorted by the small proportion of individuals with a very high level of wealth. The measure presented in the following sections is the median, where half the population lies above and half below this value. Median estimated net financial wealth of all individuals aged 50 and over in England was £12,000 in 2002 and 87 per cent had net financial wealth greater than zero. Individuals aged 50 to 54 were more likely than older age groups to have no wealth; 78 per cent had net financial wealth greater than zero.

Figure **10.4**

Median net financial wealth:[1] by age and sex, 2002

England

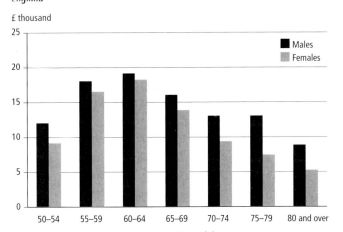

£ thousand

1 Represents savings plus investments minus debt.

Source: The 2002 English Longitudinal Study of Ageing

Median net financial wealth was highest for people aged 60 to 64 and lowest for those aged 80 and over, £19,100 compared with £6,100 (Figure 10.4). Men had greater wealth than women in all age groups, the differences being most noticeable in the 70 and over age groups. In the whole population aged 50 and over, the median net financial wealth for men was £14,400 compared with £10,500 for women.

Data from a different survey covering the 50 to 69 age group suggests there is a correlation between the level of educational attainment and net financial wealth. For individuals aged 50 to 54, median net financial wealth in 2002 was £23,000 for those with a degree compared with £13,000 for those with academic qualifications at a lower level and £1,500 for those

Figure **10.5**

Median net financial wealth: by age and education, 2002

Great Britain

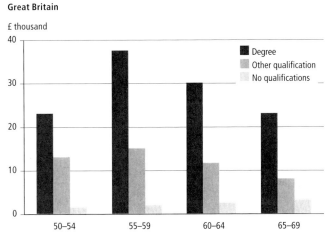

£ thousand

Source: Factors affecting the labour market participation of older workers, Department for Work and Pensions

with none (Figure 10.5). The gap between those with degrees and those with other or no qualifications was wider still for older age groups, the comparable figures for those aged 65 to 69 being £23,000, £8,000 and £3,100. People in the older age group were less likely to have degrees as they would have gone through the education system before the expansion of degree courses.

Net housing wealth

For most owner-occupiers, their house is the largest single asset that they own and a potential source of money in retirement. Housing assets can be used in several ways to fund retirement without sacrificing the benefits of rent-free living. Some pensioner households choose to 'trade-down', moving to a smaller house or flat, either releasing a capital sum that can be invested to provide a regular income, or moving from a mortgaged property to one that is owned outright. Alternatively, individuals can remain in their house and borrow against its value, receiving either a regular income or a lump sum through an equity release scheme. The equity release market is very small overall. Only about 1 per cent of pensioner households use these products, amounting to perhaps 0.5 per cent of all outstanding mortgage debt.

Figure **10.6**

Individuals with net housing wealth greater than zero:[1] by age and sex, 2002

England

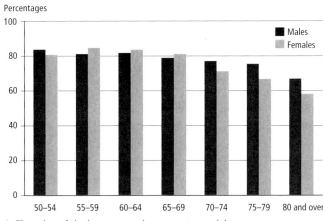

Percentages

1 The value of the house exceeds any mortgage debt.

Source: The 2002 English Longitudinal Study of Ageing

Figure 10.6 shows the percentage of individuals aged 50 and over who either own their house outright, or own a house with a value exceeding the mortgage debt. ELSA does not cover people in institutions such as nursing homes, so the figures may overstate the percentage with positive housing wealth, particularly among the oldest age groups. Over three quarters (77 per cent) of all individuals aged 50 and over had net housing wealth greater than zero. The highest percentages were in the younger age groups – at least 82 per cent of people aged 50 to 64 – and lowest in those aged 80 and over (61 per cent). There is probably a significant cohort effect underlying this age distribution – the oldest age groups are less likely to have taken advantage of the expansion of home ownership in the 1980s. Men had a higher proportion of positive net housing wealth than women in total (79 per cent of men compared with 76 per cent of women), although the reverse was true for men in the 55 to 69 age groups.

Figure **10.7**

Median net housing wealth greater than zero:[1] by age and sex, 2002

England

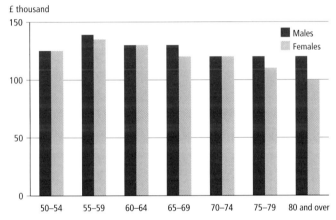

1 The value of the house exceeds any mortgage debt.
Source: The 2002 English Longitudinal Study of Ageing

Figure 10.7 shows the median value of net housing wealth for those individuals aged 50 and over who have net housing wealth greater than zero. Their median net housing wealth was £125,000. Values ranged from £110,000 in the 75 and over age groups, to £136,000 in the 55 to 59 age group. Overall, the median net housing wealth of men and women was very similar, £125,000 and £122,000 respectively. Men had median net housing wealth at least as high as women in all age groups. The largest difference was for those aged 80 and over where the median net housing wealth for men was £120,000 compared with £100,000 for women.

Total non-pension wealth

Total non-pension wealth comprises the two components already discussed, net financial wealth and net housing wealth, plus a component that is smaller for most people, physical wealth (such as business wealth, land or jewellery). In 2002, over 93 per cent of all individuals aged 50 and over in England had total non-pension wealth greater than zero. The median figure for all individuals was £126,700. It was highest

in the 55 to 59 age group for both men and women, £152,000 and £151,900 respectively, and lowest in the 80 and over age group, £96,100 for men and £60,000 for women (Figure 10.8). Averaged across all age groups, men had greater total median non-pension wealth than women (£133,600 and £119,600 respectively).

Figure **10.8**

Median total non-pension wealth: by age and sex, 2002

England

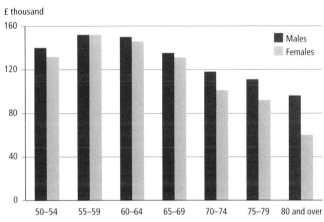

Source: The 2002 English Longitudinal Study of Ageing

Retired people aged 50 to 54 had far greater median total non-pension wealth (£250,100) than either the employed (£136,000) or self-employed (£212,000), a difference that may be partly due to a greater proportion of the retired having received a tax free lump sum as part of their pension (Figure 10.9). A different picture was apparent for individuals aged 60 to 64, where the self-employed had the greatest

Figure **10.9**

Median total non-pension wealth: by age and selected self-reported employment status, 2002

England

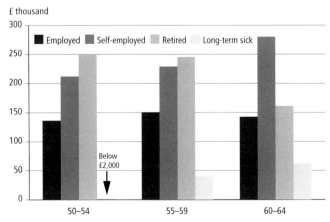

Source: The 2002 English Longitudinal Study of Ageing

median wealth (£280,000), though the retired still had a greater median wealth (£161,000) than the employed. The long-term sick group had much lower levels of median non-pension wealth (£61,700). Men had a higher median total non-pension wealth than women overall, but for self-employed women in the 50 to 54 and 55 to 59 age groups the reverse was true, though sample sizes for these groups were small and estimates may not be representative.

ELSA does not collect data on pension wealth directly though modelled estimates have been derived as explained in chapter 9. Although analyses of non-pension wealth alongside this modelled pension wealth are not yet available, non-pension wealth can be analysed according to the pension status of the individual. People aged between 50 and state pension age in work and currently contributing to a private pension had median total non-pension wealth of £164,000 (Figure 10.10). This was slightly higher than the comparable figures for those who had a previous private pension, which includes those now drawing an income from that pension. It is considerably higher than for those who had never been members of a private pension scheme, whose median total non-pension wealth was £104,500 for those in paid work and £36,000 for others. This suggests that those with the least pension provision also have less in other forms of assets to draw on in retirement.

Figure **10.10**

Median total non-pension wealth:[1] by whether currently in paid work[2] and pension status, 2002

England

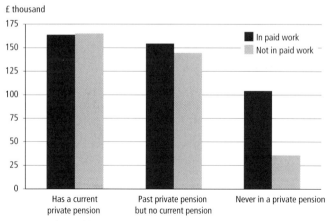

£ thousand

1 For people aged between 50 and state pension age.
2 Includes those in paid employment or self-employment and those who report waiting to take up paid work.

Source: The 2002 English Longitudinal Study of Ageing

Inheritance

An individual's resources in retirement can be increased by receiving an inheritance. The expectation of a large inheritance in the future may also influence saving behaviour. A special survey carried out by HM Revenue and Customs of estates passing through probate in 2000/01 suggests that 1.3 million bequests were made from these estates, around 1.1 million to individuals and the remainder to charities or other bodies. The average value of bequests to individuals was around £35,000, but this average conceals a wide distribution – a fifth were under £1,000, over half were under £10,000 and less than a tenth were over £100,000. The survey excluded those estates that did not go through probate, about half of the total; bequests from these must be low value as most such estates had total assets under £5,000.

The following analyses from ELSA suggest that people's *expectations* of receiving an inheritance are generally in line with this reality. Very few people expect to receive an inheritance of £100,000 or more over the next ten years, and the average estimated likelihood of receiving a large inheritance increases with current wealth, suggesting little redistribution of wealth between successive generations.

Looking at people aged 50 to 59, for the poorest fifth (by wealth) the average estimated likelihood of not receiving any inheritance is thought to be 58 per cent and the average likelihood of receiving any inheritance over the next ten years is thought to be 19 per cent (Figure 10.11). For those in the top fifth, the likelihood of not receiving any inheritance is thought to be 36 per cent and the average likelihood of receiving any inheritance over the next ten years is thought to be 38 per cent.

Figure **10.11**

Average likelihood of receiving an inheritance: by age and wealth quintile,[1] 2002

England

Percentages

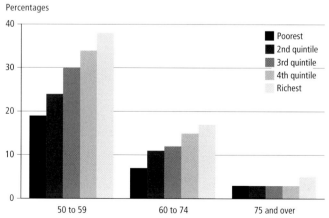

1 See Glossary for an explanation of quintiles.

Source: The 2002 English Longitudinal Study of Ageing

For individuals aged 60 to 74, their assessment of the average likelihood of receiving an inheritance ranges from 7 per cent for the poorest fifth to 17 per cent for the richest fifth. The probability of receiving no inheritance at all is 82 per cent for the poorest fifth, decreasing to 65 per cent for the richest fifth. People aged 75 and over were the least likely to expect to receive any inheritance, probably reflecting the fact that they have fewer living relatives to make such a bequest.

The larger the inheritance, the less is the expectation of receiving one. The average likelihood of someone aged 50 to 59 receiving an inheritance of at £100,000 or more over the next ten years ranges from 3 to 13 per cent between the poorest and richest wealth quintiles. The likelihood of not receiving such an inheritance is 90 per cent for the poorest quintile, reducing to 71 per cent for those in the richest quintile. For individuals aged 60 to 74, the average likelihood of receiving an inheritance of £100,000 or more ranges from 1 to 5 per cent between the poorest and richest quintiles. However, 96 per cent of the poorest fifth expect to receive no such inheritance and even in the richest fifth, 87 per cent think that they will not.

Sources and further reading

Department for Work and Pensions, Family Resources Survey.

HM Revenue and Customs website: www.hmrc.gov.uk/stats

Humphrey A, Costigan P, Pickering K, Stratford N and Barnes M (2003) *Factors affecting the labour market participation of older workers*, Department for Work and Pensions Research Report No.200.

Marmot M, Banks J, Blundell R, Lessof C and Nazroo J (Editors) (2003) *Health, wealth and lifestyles of the older population in England: The 2002 English Longitudinal Study of Ageing*, The Institute for Fiscal Studies.

Employer pension provision

- In 2003, 52 per cent of organisations provided some type of pension or access to pensions, compared with 29 per cent in 2000. The expansion was partly driven by the introduction of stakeholder pensions.

- 85 per cent of organisations with 1,000 or more employees provided an occupational scheme in 2003 compared with less than 15 per cent of those with fewer than 20 employees.

- 59 per cent of open defined benefit schemes and 71 per cent of closed defined benefit schemes were founded before 1980, compared with only 17 per cent of open defined contribution schemes.

- There were an estimated 18,100 private sector defined benefit occupational schemes in 2004 compared with an estimated 34,700 in 2000.

- The overall number of defined contribution schemes increased from an estimated 62,600 in 2000 to 70,900 in 2004.

- Manufacturing was the most likely of the industry sectors to provide access to some form of pension (76 per cent), and also had the highest proportion of businesses offering occupational pensions (13 per cent).

Chapter 11

This chapter looks at pensions from the business/employer perspective and examines the type of pension provision made by employers. The first section covers the development of employer pension provision in the private sector, focusing particularly on recent shifts in the type of provision offered. The chapter then looks at provision by industry in the private sector and, briefly, at provision in the public sector.

Background

Employer pension provision developed steadily through the 1950s, 1960s and into the 1970s. A number of regulatory changes since the 1970s have brought about an increase in the benefits that pension schemes, particularly defined benefit schemes contracted out of the state second pension system (see Glossary), must provide.

Virtually all provision was through occupational schemes until 1988 when personal pensions were established, opening the way for different types of employer pension provision such as group personal pensions. The introduction of stakeholder pensions (see Glossary) in 2001 gave employers another option. Organisations that have more than five employees and that offer no other pension provision are required to provide access to a stakeholder pension scheme.

Changes in the extent and type of pension provision offered by employers partly reflect developments in the legal and regulatory environment such as those described above. They also reflect the economic environment and cost pressures faced by employers, and specifically the cost of pension provision.

When considering the cost, and in particular who bears the risk, of different types of provision, a key distinction is between defined benefit occupational schemes on the one hand, and defined contribution occupational schemes and personal or stakeholder pensions on the other (see box).

Development of employer provision in the private sector

Figure 11.1 gives an analysis of private sector occupational schemes by their date of foundation. Where schemes have merged the foundation date is that of the earliest predecessor. Occupational pension schemes may be open, closed, frozen or winding up (see 'status of pension scheme' in the Glossary). Figure 11.1 shows open and closed schemes and also gives an indication of the change in the balance between defined benefit and defined contribution schemes being established by private sector employers.

Defined benefit schemes are generally older than defined contribution schemes. Many of these schemes have their origins in the middle of the 20th century; 59 per cent of open defined benefit schemes and 71 per cent of closed defined benefit schemes were founded before 1980. By comparison only 17 per cent of open defined contribution schemes were founded before 1980, and 36 per cent date from 2000 or later. The figures are based on responses from schemes with 12 or more members; the small excluded schemes account for only a small proportion of membership, as discussed in the next paragraph.

Defined benefit and defined contribution schemes

A *defined benefit pension scheme* – also known as a salary related scheme – has rules that specify the benefits to be paid. In defined benefit schemes almost all the risks of operation – both favourable and adverse – fall onto the pension scheme and thus the sponsoring employer, who typically bears the balance of the cost (that is, all of the cost once any employees' contributions have been allowed for). Thus if people live longer in retirement than assumed, the cost of paying pensions for more years is borne by the pension scheme; if returns on investment are lower than assumed, the shortfall is met by the pension scheme; if salary growth is higher than assumed, then the pension scheme has to meet the higher benefit payments. However the employee bears the risk of the pension scheme being wound up with insufficient funds to meet its liabilities if

the sponsoring employer becomes insolvent and is unable to pay the debt. Recent legislation has introduced some protection for the interests of members in these circumstances.

A *defined contribution pension scheme* has benefits that are determined by the contributions paid into the scheme and the investment return on those contributions.

Under defined contribution arrangements the level of an individual's pension depends on the value of their accrued pension fund at retirement. In defined contribution occupational pension schemes this will be their share of the collective fund; in personal or stakeholder pensions each individual has their own fund. In either case the individual member carries the risks.

Figure **11.1**

Foundation dates of private sector occupational pension schemes:[1] by status and benefit structure[2]

United Kingdom

Percentages

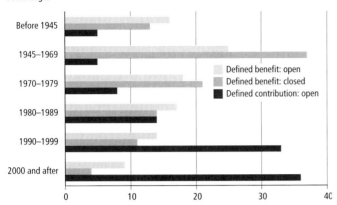

1 Schemes with 12 or more members only.
2 Data for closed defined contribution schemes are not considered reliable enough to publish.

Source: **Occupational Pension Schemes Survey 2004,** *Government Actuary's Department*

The size structure of occupational pension schemes is highly skewed, with a small number of large schemes and a much larger number of small schemes. In terms of the membership, nearly all the members belong to large schemes. In 2004, 83 per cent of open and closed private sector schemes had fewer than 12 members but these small schemes accounted for only 4 per cent of active members; 92 per cent of schemes had fewer than 100 members, accounting for only 7 per cent of total membership (Figure 11.2). At the other extreme,

Figure **11.2**

Distribution of number, and active membership, of private sector occupational pension schemes:[1] by total membership size, 2004

United Kingdom

Percentages

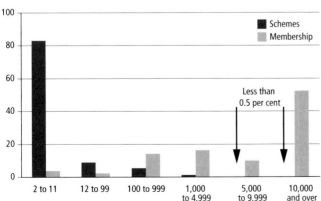

1 Open and closed schemes only.

Source: **Occupational Pension Schemes Survey 2004,** *Government Actuary's Department*

53 per cent of active membership was in the small number of very large schemes of over 10,000 members, which are associated with large employers. This skewed distribution should be borne in mind when examining the pattern of pension provision by employers presented in the following analyses.

Pension provision by private sector employers has expanded and become more diverse since 2000. Much of the expanded provision has been in the form of defined contribution arrangements, and partly driven by the introduction of stakeholder pensions. In 2003, 52 per cent of organisations provided some type of pension or access to pensions, compared with 29 per cent in 2000 (Table 11.3). The proportion of all employers offering occupational pensions was unchanged at 7 per cent, while those offering group personal pensions rose from 9 to 12 per cent. Stakeholder pensions, which did not exist in 2000, were the most common form of provision offered in 2003. Around 35 per cent of organisations provided access to stakeholder pensions in 2003, either alone or in conjunction with another type of provision, although only 5 per cent contributed to them.

Pension provision increases with size of organisation, in particular provision of an occupational scheme. Although pension provision is low in small businesses, most employment in the United Kingdom is in large companies where access to pension provision is greater. In 2003, 68 per cent of organisations with between 500 and 999 employees provided an occupational scheme and 85 per cent of those with 1,000 or more employees, compared with less than 15 per cent of those with fewer than 20 employees. Only 32 per cent of businesses with fewer than five employees had any pension provision while almost all businesses with 20 or more employees offered some form of pension provision. Among the smaller organisations, particularly those with between 5 and 12 employees, a significant minority reported making no provision, despite the requirement to do so that came into force after the introduction of stakeholder pensions. This may have been because they had not yet complied but could also result from misreporting.

Among companies offering any provision, around 27 per cent provided access to more than one type of pension in 2003, up from 14 per cent in 2000. Nearly all incidences of multiple provision involved a combination of stakeholder pension along with one or more other forms. Among companies providing occupational schemes, the incidence of multiple schemes also grew. In 2000, 92 per cent of companies offering occupational provision offered only one scheme, whereas by 2003, 71 per cent did so, while 27 per cent ran two schemes and 2 per cent three or more schemes.

Table 11.3

Incidence of pension provision: by size of organisation,[1] 2000 and 2003

Great Britain   Percentages

	2000	2003								
			Size of organisation (number of employees)							
	All	All	1–4	5–12	13–19	20–49	50–99	100–499	500–999	1,000 and over
Occupational scheme[2]	7	7	3	7	12	19	32	33	68	85
of which: open occupational scheme	..	4	-	2	9	11	17	24	46	59
Group personal pension	9	12	7	12	19	35	45	56	48	47
Contributions to personal pensions	17	15	12	17	14	25	27	32	23	25
Access to stakeholder pensions	.	35	14	64	81	85	64	65	63	63
of which: access and contributions to stakeholder pensions	.	5	3	4	15	15	15	19	11	21
Any provision	29	52	32	78	95	98	98	99	100	100
No provision	71	48	68	22	5	2	2	1	0	0

1 Employers may have more than one type of pension scheme, so percentages may add up to more than 100 per cent.
2 Occupational schemes include open, closed and frozen schemes.

Source: Employers' Pension Provision Survey 2000 and 2003, Department for Work and Pensions

Focusing on the numbers of occupational pension schemes (rather than companies offering such schemes) there have been recent changes within this type of provision, in particular a shift towards defined contribution rather than defined benefit type schemes.

There were an estimated 18,100 private sector defined benefit occupational schemes in 2004 compared with an estimated 34,700 in 2000 (Table 11.4). Most of the fall in numbers

occurred in schemes that were open. By 2004 about a third of defined benefit schemes, but two thirds of defined contribution schemes, were open to new members. The overall number of defined contribution schemes increased from an estimated 62,600 in 2000 to 70,900 in 2004.

Part of the shift from defined benefit to defined contribution schemes has involved the increased identification of 'sectionalised' schemes. Sectionalised schemes are those that

Table 11.4

UK private sector occupational pension schemes: by status[1] and benefit type, 2000 and 2004

United Kingdom   Number

	Defined benefit		Defined contribution		Total[2]	
	2000	2004	2000	2004	2000	2004
Open	17,900	6,300	43,700	46,800	62,100	54,000
Closed	11,200	8,700	17,700	10,700	29,000	19,500
Frozen	5,600	3,200	1,200	13,400	6,800	16,600
Total	**34,700**	**18,100**	**62,600**	**70,900**	**97,900**	**90,100**

1 Excludes schemes that are winding up.
2 Includes a small number of hybrid or sectionalised schemes in both years.

Source: Occupational Pension Schemes Survey 2004, Government Actuary's Department

offer different benefits to different groups of members within the same scheme, or that segregate the rights of different groups of members so as to account better for the costs arising from each group. Such schemes were not separately identified in the 2000 survey of occupational schemes as the numbers were thought to be very small. About 1,100 sectionalised schemes were identified in 2004 – these are included in the total column in Table 11.4. The majority, 61 per cent, were those where defined benefit sections had been closed to new members and defined contribution sections opened; a further 12 per cent had both defined benefit and defined contribution sections running in tandem; while the remaining 27 per cent were still wholly defined benefit, or all sections were closed.

Private sector provision by industry

The structure of the UK economy has changed from the 1950s and 1960s, when employer pension provision was developing, with manufacturing industry declining in importance and the service sector growing, particularly finance and business related services. The changes in the economy and in type of pension products are reflected in the employer pension provision on offer.

Table 11.5 shows the proportion of private sector organisations providing pensions within selected industry sectors. Manufacturing businesses were most likely to provide access to some form of pension (76 per cent), and this sector also had the highest proportion of businesses offering

occupational pensions (13 per cent). By contrast only 3 per cent of those in banking, finance and business services, for example, offered occupational pensions. This sector includes a very large number of small organisations offering a wide variety of financial, business and facilities management services. Organisations in the construction industry and in other services were least likely to provide any form of pension access.

The variation between industry sectors to some extent reflects differences in size of organisation – manufacturing firms tend to be larger than average, and as already shown larger organisations are more likely to offer occupational schemes than are smaller ones. It also reflects differences in the age structure of organisations within the sector. Manufacturing firms are more likely to be long established, and older organisations are more likely to offer occupational provision (12 per cent of those established 20 or more years ago) than are more recent ones (1 per cent of those established 2 to 4 years ago).

Public sector provision

All public sector employers offer pension provision, and virtually all provision is through defined benefit occupational schemes, though alternatives such as stakeholder pensions may also be offered. The policy, regulatory and financial framework for public sector schemes differs in some respects from that for private sector schemes and has been subject to fewer changes.

Table 11.5

Pension provision: by industry sector, 2003

Great Britain

Percentages

	Non - providers	Providers				
		Occupational pension	Group personal pension	Personal pension	Stakeholder pension	Any pension
Industry sector						
Manufacturing	24	13	19	22	48	76
Construction	62	7	12	7	32	38
Retail, distribution, hotels and catering	50	11	12	10	36	50
Transport and communications	57	3	10	7	38	43
Banking, finance and business services	46	3	13	20	29	54
Education and health	34	12	12	14	59	66
Other services	70	3	5	6	29	30
All sectors[1]	48	7	12	15	35	52

1 Includes agriculture and fishing, and energy and water sectors, which are not shown separately because of small sample sizes.

Source: Employers' Pension Provision Survey 2003, Department for Work and Pensions

Public sector schemes include those for the civil service, armed forces, teachers, National Health Service staff, local authority employees, police officers and firefighters. There were 338 UK public sector pension schemes in 2004, little changed from the 324 recorded in 2000 (Figure 11.6). Around 78 per cent were open schemes and 17 per cent were frozen, almost all of the latter being the schemes for former colonial civil servants. Every local authority, police force, and fire and rescue service is treated as having its own separate scheme in these statistics, although in practice there is one nationwide set of rules for each of these three main bodies. Public sector schemes tend to be large: around a third of all schemes had membership of 10,000 or over; and nearly two thirds membership of 1,000 or over.

Figure **11.6**

Public sector pension schemes: by membership size, 2000 and 2004

United Kingdom

Numbers

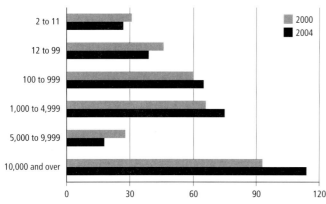

Source: Occupational Pension Schemes Survey 2000 and 2004, *Government Actuary's Department*

Sources and further reading

Department for Work and Pensions (2003), Employers' Pension Provision Survey.

Government Actuary's Department (2004), Occupational Pension Schemes Survey.

National Association of Pension Funds Annual Survey (2004).

Pension fund investment

- Total income of self-administered pension funds rose to £50.8 billion in 2004, while total expenditure was £39.0 billion.

- Total payments by self-administered pension funds to members and their dependants have increased steadily from £6.5 billion in 1984 to £33.1 billion in 2004.

- Since 1999 contributions to self-administered pension funds have increased, with employee contributions rising slowly and employer contributions showing a far greater rise.

- The value of self-administered pension funds total assets fell from £821 billion in 1999 to £620 billion in 2002, but recovered to £720 billion in 2003.

- Corporate securities accounted for 73 per cent of longer-term assets in 1990, rising to 78 per cent in 1996 and falling to 69 per cent in 2002.

- Pension fund holdings of UK equities fell from 61 per cent of corporate securities in 1999 to 39 per cent in 2003, with offsetting rises in the share of mutual funds and UK corporate bonds.

This chapter looks at pension fund finances, covering income, expenditure and investment. Data limitations mean that the analysis only covers self-administered occupational pension funds, which are funds that carry out their own investment using internal or external investment managers. These funds may be associated with either private sector or public sector funded pension schemes – see box for an explanation of schemes and funds.

Self-administered pension funds are likely to account for around 70 per cent of total occupational pension investment, with the rest accounted for by insured schemes. Insured schemes, which are generally smaller than self-administered schemes, secure their members' retirement benefits through investment in insurance policies. The investment funds for these insured pension schemes are pooled with other long-term assets – both personal pensions and other types of insurance company business – and the pension assets are not identified separately by insurance companies.

Most self-administered pension funds are associated with occupational schemes offering some form of defined benefit pension, where each member's pension is defined by rules involving salary levels and length of service. Entitlement builds up over many years and the scheme's ability to pay pensions is dependent on the size of the fund being sufficient to meet those liabilities. Other self-administered funds are associated with defined contribution schemes, where pension benefits

depend on the size of the pension fund on retirement. In these cases, changes in the value of the fund will affect the pensions payable to members on retirement.

Total income and expenditure

Figure 12.1 shows the growth in total income and expenditure for self-administered pension funds. Total income for self-administered pension funds consists of employers' and

Figure **12.1**

Self-administered pension funds: total income and expenditure
United Kingdom

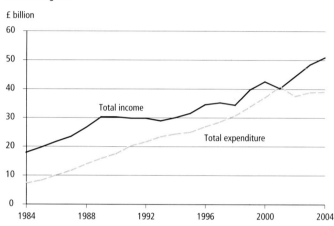

Source: Survey of self-administered pension funds, Office for National Statistics

---

Pension schemes and pension funds

A pension *scheme* is an arrangement to provide benefits on retirement. An occupational scheme is organised by an employer, or on behalf of a group of employers, to provide benefits for one or more employees. The scheme is defined by a set of rules concerning the level of contributions, what benefits are paid out and when, membership eligibility, etc.

Contributions made to the pension schemes are invested in a pension *fund* and the proceeds from that fund provide the benefits paid out on retirement. A pension fund can be thought of as the assets – the pot of money – associated with a pension scheme. The relationship between pension schemes and pension funds may be:

* One-to-one: a scheme's assets are invested in a single fund and the entire fund belongs to that scheme;

* Many-to-one: a group of schemes run by a single employer or a group of employers, with different rates

of contributions and benefits for different groups of employees, pooling their assets in one fund;

* One-to-many: this arrangement is not so common, but one large example is the local government scheme. There is one scheme, or set of rules, for all local government employees, with each local authority or small group of local authorities having its own fund. This local government scheme is the only major public sector scheme that is funded in this way. Other public sector schemes are run on an unfunded basis, meaning that there is no pot of money associated with the schemes; pension payments are paid out of current revenues.

A personal pension scheme is an arrangement between an individual and a financial institution, though such schemes may also be facilitated or sponsored by employers. The individual's contribution to their scheme, either separately or in a group personal pension, forms the basis of their pension fund.

employees' contributions, income from rent, interest and dividends, and inward transfer payments. Total income rose from £17.8 billion in 1984 to £50.8 billion in 2004, although there was little growth between 1989 and 1995. Part of the increase from 1999 reflects increases in inward transfer payments. These are payments made from one pension fund to another in lieu of benefits that have accrued to the transferring member or members to enable the receiving pension arrangement to provide alternative benefits. Transfers may occur when people change employers or when pension schemes are taken over en bloc.

Total expenditure for pension funds is made up of payments to members and their dependants; transfers out to other pension schemes; and other expenditure, which is mainly for administration. Expenditure rose steadily from £7.3 billion in 1984 to a peak of £40.8 billion in 2001 when transfer out payments peaked at almost £8 billion. Expenditure fell back to around £39 billion in 2003 and 2004. The composition of expenditure and income is discussed in more detail in the next sections.

Net income – the balance between total income and expenditure – had been falling since the late 1980s, reducing the surplus available for investment. It has risen since 2001, as employers' contributions rose sharply.

Expenditure

Total payments to members and their dependants, which cover pensions, lump sums on retirement and death benefits, have increased steadily from £6.5 billion in 1984 to £33.1 billion in 2004 (Figure 12.2). The pensions element, on average over the period from 1984 to 2004, accounted for 82 per cent of total payments and 66 per cent of total expenditure.

This rise in payments to members is largely the impact of the increasing maturity of pension schemes as employees who joined pension schemes in the 1950s and 1960s, a period when pension scheme membership rose, began to enter retirement. In addition, the *1986 Finance Act* required pension funds to identify whether, given certain actuarial assumptions (see Glossary) they had a surplus of 5 per cent or more, and to take action to remove the surplus within five years or else lose some of their tax exempt status. In some cases the surpluses were used to fund early retirement.

A further factor is that in 1988 pension schemes became responsible for indexation of Guaranteed Minimum Pension payments by up to 3 per cent. The *Pension Act 1995* introduced limited price indexation of up to 5 per cent for occupational pension payments from 1997.

Other expenditure includes transfer payments to other pension funds and administrative costs. Transfer payments rose from around £600 million in 1984 to almost £4 billion in 1991, before declining to around £2 billion in 1995. These payments then rose to peak at almost £8 billion in 2001.

Income

Figure 12.3 breaks down total income into contributions and investment income. UK pension funds have tended to invest heavily in equities and were badly hit by the stock market slump of 1973/74. The recovery in the equity markets through the 1980s and into the 1990s contributed to the rise in income from rents, dividends and interest up to 1997. Since 2000, investment income has fallen reflecting the downturn of the equity market.

Figure **12.2**

Self-administered pension funds: expenditure
United Kingdom

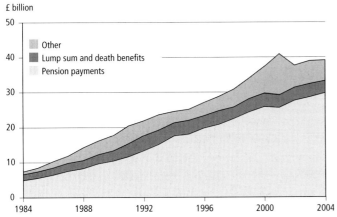

Source: Survey of self-administered pension funds, Office for National Statistics

Figure **12.3**

Self-administered pension funds: income
United Kingdom

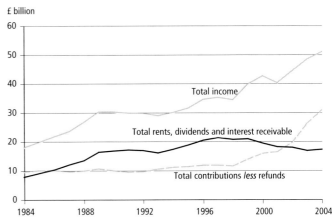

Source: Survey of self-administered pension funds, Office for National Statistics

The figures for aggregate pension contributions presented in chapter 8 include an element of estimation as discussed. Contributions to self-administered pension funds are thought to be one of the more reliable components of these aggregates, as these funds are able to provide figures for new contributions net of transfers. They are also able to provide a breakdown between employers' and employees' contributions. Their total contribution income, which had risen in the late 1970s to help shore up pension finances post-1974, was more or less flat from 1980 until the late 1990s as pension schemes acted to reduce their surpluses by lowering contribution rates and granting contributions holidays. For example, statistics from HM Revenue and Customs show that the number of pension schemes reporting surpluses of over 5 per cent rose to over 1,000 in the three years 1995/96 to 1997/98 and has fallen since then.

The reduction of schemes in surplus and of those on contribution holidays is reflected in the growth in contributions in recent years. These have been rising since 1999 as pension schemes attempt to rebuild their finances in the light of reduced investment returns and the increasing longevity of retirees.

Looking at contributions in more detail, employees' contributions rose slowly from 1984 to 1992, fell back slightly to 1998 and have risen slowly since 1998 (Figure 12.4). The rise in normal contributions from employers is larger, from £4.4 billion in 1992 to £17.6 billion in 2004. Employers' additional contributions, which averaged around £1.2 billion between 1992 and 1998, started to increase from 1999 and rose sharply from 2001 to reach almost £8 billion in 2004 as pension schemes attempted to reduce their deficits. These additional contributions are payments made by employers, over and above normal payments, to reduce funding deficits or to meet additional costs as required by the scheme rules. The distinction between normal and additional contributions has become blurred as, in some pension schemes, the employer pays the balance of the cost between employees' contributions and the funding required for the scheme.

New data from the survey of self-administered pension funds, collected for the first time in 2004, show that total contributions to defined benefit schemes are substantially greater than those to defined contribution schemes, accounting for over 90 per cent of employers' contributions. However the position is thought to be different for insured schemes, where data from the Association of British Insurers show that most of the contributions are to defined contribution schemes rather than defined benefit schemes. As contributions to insured schemes are smaller, taking both self-administered and insured together, contributions to defined benefit schemes still predominate. This is consistent with the position for

Figure **12.4**

Self-administered pension funds: contributions
United Kingdom

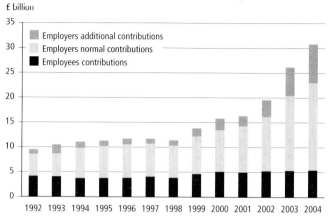

Source: Survey of self-administered pension funds, Office for National Statistics

membership; while there has been a move away from defined benefit schemes, as discussed in chapter 11, the bulk of occupational scheme membership is still in these schemes.

Asset holdings

The composition of pension fund asset holdings is shown in Figure 12.5. Short-term assets such as cash form a very small part of the total. Longer-term assets comprise corporate securities; public sector securities; and other assets, which include fixed assets (buildings, land and machinery), holdings in insurance managed funds, and holdings of overseas government securities. Within other assets, the main growth area has been holdings of insurance managed funds (where insurance companies offer participation in pooled funds).

Figure **12.5**

Self-administered pension funds: asset holdings at market values
United Kingdom

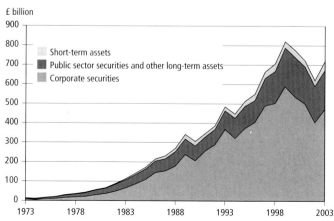

Source: Survey of self-administered pension funds, Office for National Statistics

Pension fund holdings of these funds have risen from £13 billion in 1997 to £43 billion in 2003.

The bulk of longer-term assets comprise corporate securities, which are UK and overseas equities, corporate bonds and mutual funds. Corporate securities accounted for 73 per cent of longer-term assets in 1990, rising to 78 per cent in 1996 and falling to 69 per cent in 2002. The growth in the UK stock market through the 1980s and 1990s, with an average real rate of return on UK equities of 13 per cent between 1974 and 2000, led to a significant increase in pension fund assets. The downturn in the stock market from early 2000 significantly affected the value of pension funds and their investments. The value of total assets fell from £821 billion in 1999 to £620 billion in 2002, but recovered to £720 billion in 2003.

equities, changes to accounting standards for reporting pension scheme deficits and the maturing and closure of pension schemes to new members will have impacted on fund investment decisions. As pension schemes mature, they are likely to want to reduce their exposure to equities and their associated risks, and to move to bonds.

Figure 12.7 illustrates the shift in the allocation of funds between 1999 and 2003. Pension fund holdings of UK equities fell from 61 per cent of corporate securities in 1999 to 39 per cent in 2003; mutual funds rose from 11 per cent in 1999 to 24 per cent in 2003; and UK corporate bonds rose from 1.5 per cent in 1999 to 8 per cent in 2003. Overseas securities (shares and corporate bonds) rose from 26 per cent of corporate securities in 1999 to 29 per cent in 2003.

Figure **12.6**

Self-administered pension funds: holdings of corporate securities

United Kingdom

£ billion

Source: Survey of self-administered pension funds, Office for National Statistics

A breakdown of corporate securities is shown in Figure 12.6. UK equities remained the main investment vehicle for pension funds, although the value of these holdings has dropped sharply since 1999. While this partly reflects the fall and subsequent weakness of UK equities, there has also been a shift to other types of investment. Holdings of overseas securities (predominantly shares) are the second largest component of corporate securities and have maintained their share of pension fund investments. There has been some movement into UK corporate bonds, although they remain a small part of total corporate securities. The main rise in holdings has been in mutual funds, which include unit trusts and investment trusts, open ended investment companies and common investment funds.

A number of factors have encouraged pension funds to review their investment strategy. In addition to the adjustment in

Figure **12.7**

Self-administered pension funds: share of corporate securities, 1999 and 2003

United Kingdom

Percentages

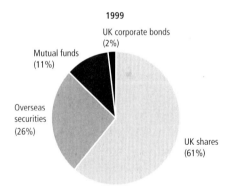

Total value of corporate securities = £586 billion

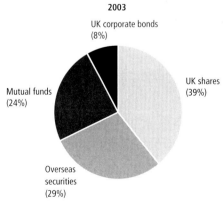

Total value of corporate securities = £473 billion

Source: Survey of self-administered pension funds, Office for National Statistics

Figure **12.8**

Beneficial ownership of UK shares, 1992 and 2004

United Kingdom

Percentages

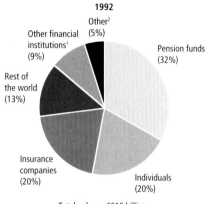

1992

Other[2] (5%)

Other financial institutions[1] (9%)

Rest of the world (13%)

Pension funds (32%)

Insurance companies (20%)

Individuals (20%)

Total value = £616 billion

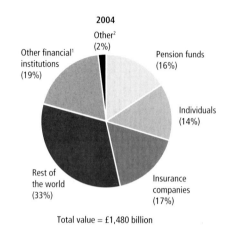

2004

Other[2] (2%)

Other financial[1] institutions (19%)

Pension funds (16%)

Individuals (14%)

Rest of the world (33%)

Insurance companies (17%)

Total value = £1,480 billion

1 'Other financial institutions' includes: unit trusts, investment trusts and banks.
2 'Other' includes: private non-financial companies, public sector, charities and churches.

Source: Share Ownership Report, Office for National Statistics

The importance of pension funds relative to other sectors' holdings of UK shares can be illustrated by results from the share ownership survey for 2004. The proportion of UK shares listed on the London Stock Exchange held by pension funds has been on a downward trend since 1993, falling from 32 per cent in 1992 to 16 per cent in 2004 (Figure 12.8). Insurance company holdings represent both their pension business and

their other long-term business – separate data is not available. Their share increased slightly from 20 per cent in 1992 to a peak of 23.5 per cent in 1997 then fell to 17 per cent in 2004. Despite this downward trend, insurance companies and pension funds are the two largest UK holders of UK shares, with foreign investors (holding 33 per cent) the largest holders overall.

Sources

Office for National Statistics (2005) *Survey of self-administered pension funds.*

Share ownership survey, Office for National Statistics. A copy of the *Share Ownership Report* is available at nswebcopy/downloads/theme_economy/shareOwnership2004.pdf

Pensions and the National Accounts

- The National Accounts measures of pension contributions cover those to schemes classified as 'social' insurance schemes, and count investment income as part of employee contributions.

- On National Accounts definitions, employer social contributions grew from £18.7 billion to £37.8 billion between 1999 and 2004, while employee social contributions rose from £30.8 billion to £31.6 billion.

- In 2004, household assets held in life assurance and pension funds reserves were £1,630 billion; in cash terms this was the same as at the peak in 1999.

- Pension assets make up half (51 per cent) of total household financial assets, and 28 per cent of net household wealth.

- State pensions are paid by the Government from the National Insurance Fund (NIF) with total payments in 2004 of £48 billion.

- The state pension scheme represented an estimated liability of £1,128 billion to the Government in 2002.

- Tax relief on pension contributions increased from £10.6 billion in 1998/99 to £16.6 billion in 2003/04, and tax received on pension payments from £6.1 billion to £8.0 billion.

Chapter 13

The National Accounts

This chapter considers the ways in which transactions related to pension provision are incorporated in the National Accounts and contribute to aggregate measures such as Gross Domestic Product (GDP see Glossary) and the household saving ratio. As required by EU Regulation, the national accounts treatment adopted in the United Kingdom is that defined by the European System of Accounts 1995 (ESA95), which is based on the international System of National Accounts 1993 (SNA93). An aim of the National Accounts is to capture various economic transactions in a standardised form and present them in a way that identifies both their whole economy impact and their 'sectoral' impact. The discussion and information in this chapter is organised according to the sectoral perspective, which is also consistent with the broader framework for pension statistics discussed in the Introduction.

In general terms, households are the main beneficiaries of pension schemes; they interact with the corporate sector (both financial and non-financial) as providers of both occupational and personal pensions; and with the government sector through National Insurance contributions, the state pension scheme and public sector employee occupational schemes. The discussion of the government sector also includes its role in fostering private provision.

Households

The household sector is the beneficiary of nearly all pension payments, and most pension scheme transactions involve the household sector. The other beneficiaries are UK households resident overseas who, in the National Accounts, are defined as belonging to the 'rest of the world' sector. The household sector includes non-profit institutions serving households (such as charities); the figures cannot be separated.

The National Accounts distinguishes between employer and employee contributions. As part of the remuneration for labour, these contributions are part of the national accounts aggregate 'compensation of employees'. In accordance with the 'accruals approach', these contributions are recorded when the labour takes place rather than when the pensions are actually paid on and after retirement. Pension contributions are therefore part of the income measure of GDP[1] and a component of the aggregate measure of household revenue that underpins the calculation of saving and the saving ratio.

Some pension flows are classified within the National Accounts as social contributions or social benefits (pensions in payment). 'Social' is a national accounts concept that allows the identification of transactions related to the provision of 'insurance' (through both the public and private sectors) for

events and circumstances such as illness and unemployment as well as retirement. All occupational and employer-sponsored personal pensions are defined as 'social' insurance schemes. Other personal pensions are not regarded as social schemes but as the purchase of a saving instrument, in the same way as investing money in an Individual Savings Account is regarded as the purchase of a saving instrument.

The main national accounts measures of private pension contributions are 'social contributions to private funded pension schemes', and are shown on Figure 13.1. The chart illustrates the contrasting behaviour of employees' and employers' contributions, with employees' contributions fairly flat in recent years, but employers' contributions growing quickly following the need to make special contributions to make up shortfalls in defined benefit funds (see chapter 8). Between 1999 and 2004 employers' social contributions grew from £18.7 billion to £37.8 billion, while employees' social contributions went up from £30.8 billion to £31.6 billion.

Figure **13.1**

Social contributions by households and NPISHs[1] to funded pension schemes

United Kingdom

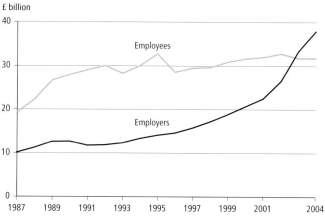

1 Non-profit institutions serving households sector in National Accounts. This includes charities, religious organisations, trade unions, some higher education institutions and friendly societies that provide goods and services to households free, or at prices that are not economically significant.

Source: Office for National Statistics

There are a number of differences between these national accounts estimates of pension contributions and those presented in chapter 8. In the main these differences relate to an alternative and more complicated treatment of personal pensions, and to the inclusion in employees' contributions of a large component for the interest and dividend income earned on the stock of pension contributions. For the purposes of National Accounts this stock and the investment return on it is treated as owned by the household sector.

An associated measure used primarily for economic analysis is the household saving ratio. This measure provides a broad indication of the difference between household income and consumption, calculated as a percentage of total household income. Figure 13.2 shows the saving ratio over the full period for which consistent figures are available.

Figure **13.2**

Household saving ratio[1]

United Kingdom

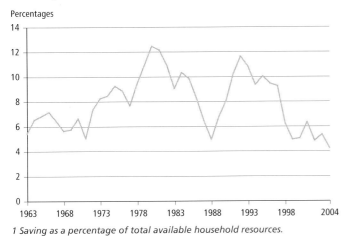

1 Saving as a percentage of total available household resources.

Source: Office for National Statistics

The saving ratio indicates a relatively long period of low saving out of income. The ratio has been below 6 per cent in five of the last six years; since the start of the 1970s it has only fallen below 6 per cent on two other occasions (although before 1970 lower outturns were more common).

Neither the overall level of pension contributions nor the saving ratio provides a reliable measure of the strength or weakness of pension savings and investments. Measures based on pension contributions are not necessarily indicative of changes in pension coverage, entitlement, or the actual benefits households expect to receive on retirement. Contributions are partly determined by funding requirements and tend to increase more slowly during periods of strong investment growth. Also, the saving ratio does not take account of payments into non-financial assets that may be regarded as important sources of income on retirement, such as housing and the business assets of the self-employed.

Movements in the household saving ratio may reflect changes that have little to do with saving behaviour for retirement. Increases in debt or a reduction in accumulated wealth or assets (for example, households withdrawing equity on their houses) increase consumption without increasing income and lead to a decline in the ratio. At the same time, purchases of non-financial assets, some of which could provide income in

retirement, also increase consumption without increasing income and lead to a decline in the ratio. As a result, the household saving ratio only partly reflects overall saving in the economy, and trends in the measure may not be mirrored in total saving.

The National Accounts also includes balance sheets that provide estimates of the total financial and non-financial assets and liabilities for each sector of the economy. The household sector balance sheet includes an estimate for the total value of household wealth held in private pension funds (occupational and personal) based on the value of the assets held by insurance companies and pension funds. This total value also includes other life insurance products, as insurance companies pool the assets and the pension element is not separately identifiable.

Figure 13.3 shows total household assets held in life assurance and pension funds as a percentage of GDP. They increased rapidly relative to GDP throughout the 1990s, but dropped back sharply with the falls in equity values in the early 2000s. In 2004, household assets held in life assurance and pension funds reserves were £1,630 billion; in cash terms this was the same as at the peak in 1999.

Figure **13.3**

Household assets in life assurance and pension fund reserves as a percentage of GDP

United Kingdom

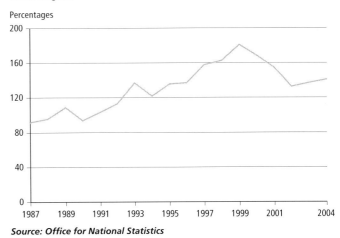

Source: Office for National Statistics

Pension assets make up half (51 per cent) of total financial assets, and 28 per cent of net household wealth (Table 13.4). Apart from other financial assets the main assets of the sector are residential buildings, which account for 55 per cent or 40 per cent after mortgages are netted off. Taking into account all liabilities, the total net worth of households and non-profit institutions serving households in 2004 is estimated at £5,810 billion.

Table **13.4**

Household sector balance sheet, 2004

United Kingdom

	£ billion	Percentage of net worth
Assets		
Financial		
Currency and deposits	860	15
Shares and other equity	500	9
Net equity in life assurance and pension funds	1,630	28
Other	190	3
Total	**3,180**	**55**
Non-financial		
Residential buildings	3,220	55
Other	610	10
Total	**3,830**	**66**
Total assets	**7,010**	**121**
Liabilities		
Loans secured on dwellings	870	-15
Other	320	-5
Total	**1,190**	**-21**
Net worth	**5,810**	**100**

Source: Office for National Statistics

Companies

Pension transactions across the corporate sector reflect two different roles of companies in pension provision:

- across all companies through their provision of occupational pensions or access to personal pensions for their employees; and

- across the financial corporations that are specialist providers of pensions.

For those in the first category, pension contributions are a cost to the corporate sector, while for those in the second category, pension contributions are income, and pensions and benefit payments are costs.

The household assets in insurance company and pension fund reserves are recorded as a liability to the insurance corporations and pension funds sector (even though the liability is shared between private non-financial corporations and financial corporations sectors). The National Accounts contains detailed information on how insurance corporations and pension funds invest the aggregate stock of reserves.

The investment activities of self-administered pension funds were discussed in chapter 12. Figure 13.5 shows the size of insurance corporations and pension funds holdings of each of the main financial assets relative to holdings by other UK institutional sectors.

Figure **13.5**

Asset holdings of insurance corporations and pension funds, and other institutions, 2004

United Kingdom

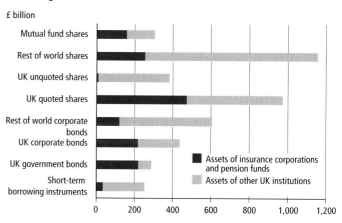

Source: Office for National Statistics

By proportion insurance companies and pension funds held the greatest share of UK government bonds (76 per cent) in 2004; they also had large holdings of UK quoted shares (49 per cent), UK corporate bonds (50 per cent) and UK mutual fund shares (52 per cent). In value terms the most important assets of insurance company and pension funds were UK quoted shares (£472 billion).

For some types of savings and pensions the assets held by the household sector are in practice identical to the liability of the insurance companies and pension funds, but this may not be the case for those types of investment where there is some form of guaranteed return, notably defined benefit occupational pension schemes (see Glossary). However, the methodology used to construct the National Accounts means that the aggregate liability of insurance companies and pension funds is assumed equal to their aggregate assets. There is therefore no official estimate of the pension fund 'shortfall' that occurs where aggregate liabilities of defined benefit schemes are higher than their associated assets. These liabilities ultimately fall on the company providing the occupational scheme, as discussed in chapter 11.

However some assessment of the impact of pension contributions on the company sector can be made. Employers' contributions to pension schemes constitute a cost to private

Figure **13.6**

Allocation of income of private non-financial corporations[1]

United Kingdom

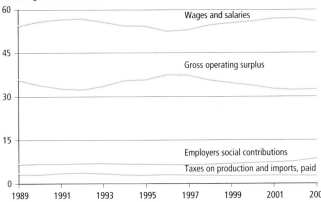

Percentage of total resources

1 *Unlike Figure 13.1, the estimate for employers social contributions here also includes the National Insurance contributions that employees pay to the government sector.*

Source: Office for National Statistics

non-financial corporations. Figure 13.6 shows the relative shares of these contributions set against wages and salaries, taxes and gross operating surplus.

In 2003, the latest year for which the full analysis of private non-financial corporations' income flows are available, 8.7 per cent of their income was paid out in employers' contributions. This includes both contributions to funded schemes and National Insurance contributions. Wages and salaries accounted for the largest share, at 56 per cent, leaving gross operating surplus at 32.6 per cent. Figure 13.6 also illustrates the recent rise in employers' contributions; between 1989 and 1999 the share of employers' contributions was stable at around 7 per cent of income; but between 1999 and 2003 that share had risen to 8.7 per cent. Gross operating surplus fell as a share of income from the mid 1990s until 2002, with wages, salaries and social contributions taking a larger share.

Government

The Government has always been the key player in the provision of UK pensions. Its most direct role is as provider of the state pension and associated 'second tier' schemes such as state second pension, and through occupational schemes for government employees; but at the same time it has sought to foster private provision through incentives using the National Insurance and tax systems.

The National Accounts provides measures of the size of government pension provision. As with occupational schemes, the state pension scheme is a social benefit. These benefits are paid by the Government from the National Insurance Fund

(NIF) with total payments in 2004 of £48 billion (out of total NIF benefits of £58 billion). In 2004, total contributions to the NIF were £77 billion. Despite the terminology National Insurance 'Fund', all NIF benefits are provided on a 'pay as you go' basis. That is, the contributions paid in any time period by the working population fund the benefits paid out in the same time period, including state pensions to the retired population. The state pension scheme is therefore described as 'unfunded'.

Most public sector occupational schemes are also unfunded, with pension payments being made out of general government revenue. Estimates for actual and imputed contributions to these schemes are given in chapter 8.

Unlike for funded occupational schemes, the National Accounts does not provide a measure of government liabilities to households arising from the state scheme or unfunded occupational pension schemes. The Government Actuary's Department estimated that the state pension scheme represented a total liability of £1,128 billion to the Government in 2002. Liabilities related to public service employment pension schemes are reported as part of the annual resource accounting process. These estimates represent pension rights that have built up during service already provided by public servants. They are not projections of pension rights likely to be accrued in the future. Table 13.7 provides estimates for the largest schemes and an overall estimate of the total liability to the Government of unfunded public service pension schemes at £460 billion.

Table **13.7**

Liabilities of unfunded public service pension schemes, 2003/04

United Kingdom	£ billion
Total	**460**
of which:	
Teachers	113
National Health Service (England and Wales)	104
Civil service	79
Armed forces	64

Source: Departmental resource accounts, various government departments; HM Treasury

Beyond its role in state pension provision, the Government has actively encouraged the taking up of private pensions, both as an alternative to second tier provision through the state second pension and as additional third tier provision. As discussed in chapter 6, those who contract out (see Glossary)

Table **13.8**

Pensions taxation and National Insurance relief

United Kingdom

£ billion

	1998/99	1999/2000	2000/01	2001/02	2002/03	2003/04
Tax relief on contributions[1]	10.6	11.5	12.3	12.9	14.5	16.6
Tax relief on investment income of funds[2]	4.0	4.0	4.1	3.7	3.1	2.6
Tax relief on lump sum payments[3]	1.4	1.5	1.4	1.4	1.5	1.5
National Insurance relief on employer contributions	2.6	3.1	3.4	3.7	4.1	5.8
Tax received on pension payments[4]	6.1	6.6	7.3	7.5	7.7	8.0

1 *Includes relief at appropriate rate on contributions from employees, employers, self-employed and other individuals.*
2 *Assuming relief at the basic rate of tax. Does not include relief on capital gains made by pension funds as data is not available.*
3 *Assuming relief at the basic rate of tax.*
4 *Assuming pension payments represent top slice of taxable income.*

Source: HM Revenue and Customs

of the state second pension pay lower National Insurance contributions. The amounts by which payments are reduced or rebated in 2004/05 are estimated by the Government Actuary's Department as £7.5 billion for those who contract out into an occupational scheme, and £3.5 billion for those who contract out using a personal or stakeholder pension. The level of these rebates broadly reflects the lower entitlement to state pension for those who contract out, though at times rebates have been set at a level to provide an additional incentive to contract out.

Tax and National Insurance relief on pension contributions and pension fund investment returns is in part an encouragement to save, though it can also be seen as an integral feature of the overall taxation system. Pensions in payment are taxed as earned income in the normal way, so relief is given on contributions and investment income to avoid double taxation over the lifetime of the individual who first saves for, then draws on, a pension.

However looking at the aggregate position on a cash flow basis, the cost of relief on contributions and investment income is currently greater than tax received on pensions paid in the same period (Table 13.8). If the ratio of pensioners to contributors increases, as is likely under current trends, the cost of tax relief may decline in real terms or as a proportion of GDP. However there are three elements of the relief that are not balanced by a charge when pension income is paid. These would continue regardless of the ratio between pensioners and contributors and represent a true benefit to the individual and cost to government:

● up to a quarter of an individual's total pension fund can be taken as a tax free lump sum on retirement;

● the highest rate of tax charged on pension income in retirement may be lower than the rate at which relief was given during working life. This is because on retirement, total income is generally lower and personal tax allowances are higher for those aged over 65; and

● National Insurance relief is given on employer contributions. Employer contributions represent a benefit to the employee. Such benefits are generally subject to National Insurance but pension contributions are exempt and National Insurance is not chargeable on private pensions in payment.

The estimates in Table 13.8 are derived from components in the table of costs of relief for approved pension schemes published by HM Revenue and Customs. The figures are not additive as there are interactions between the components and any estimate of 'overall' cost depends on assumptions on what the alternative to the current arrangements would be. The figures are subject to a wide margin of error, and do not represent the effect of changing the tax and National Insurance system as there would be significant changes in taxpayer behaviour.

Tax relief on contributions increased from £10.6 billion in 1998/99 to £16.6 billion (provisional estimate) for 2003/04, largely in line with contributions themselves, though the cost was also affected by changes in the average marginal rate at which relief was given. The fall in tax relief on the investment income of funds from around £4 billion in the three years up to 2000/01 to £2.6 billion in 2003/04 occurred mainly as a result of falling investment returns, for example lower interest rates. This component does not include a potentially large amount of relief on the capital gains accruing to funds as estimates are not available. The estimate of around £1.5 billion each year for relief given on lump sum pension payments is very broad brush. National Insurance relief on employer pension contributions rose over the whole period to reach £5.8 billion in 2003/04. The increase was particularly marked in the most recent years when the level of contributions increased rapidly as noted in earlier sections.

References

1 The income measure of GDP includes compensation of employees, which is made up of wages and salaries plus employers' pension contributions. Employees' pension contributions are paid from employees' wages or salaries and are therefore not included as a separate component in the calculation for GDP. (Although in practice in the United Kingdom the calculation involves adding an estimate of employees' contributions to a wages and salaries figure net of employees' contributions.)

Sources and further reading

HM Revenue and Customs website: http://www.hmrc.gov.uk/stats/

National Statistics website: Forrest C, Penneck P and Tily G (2004) 'Private Pensions Estimates and the National Accounts', *Economic Trends* No. 609, pp 36–46. Office for National Statistics www.statistics.gov.uk/cci/article.asp?ID=910

National Statistics website: Penneck P and Tily G (2005) 'Private pension contributions: updated estimates 1996 – 2004' http://www.statistics.gov.uk/articles/nojournal/Private_pension_estimates1996-2004.pdf

Pensions Commission, 7 July 2005, *Sectoral and National Savings: Discussion Paper.* http://www.pensionscommission.org.uk/publications/2005/sec-nat-savings.pdf

Glossary

Active member

An employee who is currently in pensionable service in an occupational pension scheme.

Actuarial assumptions/estimates/deductions

The various estimates (including assumptions related to changes in longevity, wages, inflation, returns on assets, and so on) that the actuary makes in formulating a valuation or other calculations.

Actuary

An adviser on financial questions involving probabilities relating to mortality and other contingencies.

Additional 'second tier' entitlements

The earnings-related part of the state pension over and above the basic pension, provided by the state earnings-related pension scheme (SERPS) or the state second pension (S2P).

Additional voluntary contributions

Contributions over and above a member's normal contributions into an occupational pension scheme that a member elects to pay in order to secure additional benefits.

Administrative data

Data that are a by-product of the operational activity of an organisation. This contrasts with survey data that are collected specifically for a statistical or research purpose.

Cohort life expectancy

Cohort life expectancy is calculated using the mortality rates that a particular cohort is projected to experience. For instance, the cohort life expectancy for a 65 year old in 2002 will be calculated using the mortality rate for a 65 year old in 2002, for a 66 year old in 2003, for a 67 year old in 2004, and so on.

Contracted out

This refers to a statutory arrangement under which pension schemes that meet certain conditions may contract out of the state second pension (S2P), formerly the state earnings-related pension (SERPS). The members' and employers' National Insurance contributions are reduced or rebated. Members of a contracted out pension scheme obtain rights in the pension scheme in place of additional earnings-related benefits under the state scheme. See also **Minimum contribution**.

Contribution

Payments into a pension scheme from members or employers.

Crude birth rate

The simplest overall measure of fertility in a population, given by the number of live births in a year per 1,000 mid-year population. It takes no account of the composition of the population, in particular the age and sex distribution.

Crude death rate

The basic measure of the level of mortality in a population, defined as total deaths per 1,000 mid-year population. It takes no account of any variation in mortality levels by age.

Deferred entitlement

Entitlement to a pension payable some time in the future. It can be either entitlement to a pension payable from retirement age for someone who has left the scheme or entitlement to a pension that has been deferred because retirement has been postponed beyond retirement date.

Defined benefit scheme

A pension scheme in which the rules specify the benefits to be paid – also known as a salary related scheme – some are based on final salary, some are based on average salary.

Defined contribution scheme

A pension scheme in which the benefits are determined by the contributions paid into the scheme and the investment return on those contributions – also known as a money purchase scheme.

Free standing additional voluntary contributions (FSAVC)

Contributions to a pension contract separate from an occupational pension scheme effected by an active member of that scheme. Benefits are secured with a pension provider by contributions from the member only.

Funded scheme

A scheme in which benefits are met from a fund built up in advance from contributions and investment income.

Gross Domestic Product (GDP)

The total value of economic activity in a country or region. It is measured in either current prices or real terms.

Group personal pensions

An arrangement made for the employees of a particular employer to participate in a personal pension scheme on a group basis. This is not a separate pension scheme, but merely a collecting arrangement.

Household reference person

Sometimes it is necessary to select one person in a household to indicate the general characteristics of the household. For this purpose the household reference person has replaced the head of household in all government-sponsored household surveys after 2000–01. The household reference person is identified during the interview and is either the householder (in whose name the accommodation is owned or rented) or in households with joint householders, the person with the highest income or, if both householders have the same income, the oldest householder.

Hybrid scheme

A pension scheme with elements of both defined contribution and defined benefit, for example pensions set as the better of a final salary and a money purchase basis.

Insured scheme

A scheme for which the retirement benefits are secured by insurance policies and which is administered by the insurance company.

Mean

The mean is calculated by taking the sum of all the data values and dividing by the total number of data values. Its value depends equally on all of the data, which may include outliers and so it may not represent the middle in skewed data sets.

Median

The middle point of a population with exactly the same number of data values above and below. It works well for skewed data, or data with outliers.

Minimum contribution/National Insurance rebate

Contributions payable to a contracted out personal or stakeholder pension scheme from the National Insurance Fund in respect of a member who has elected to contract out.

National Insurance rebate

See **Minimum contribution**

Non-state pension

A pension other than the state basic retirement or earnings-related pension, sometimes referred to as a private pension. Includes all occupational and personal pensions, including those for public sector employees.

Occupational pension scheme

An arrangement (other than accident or permanent health insurance) organised by an employer (or on behalf of a group of employers) to provide benefits for employees on their retirement and for their dependants on their death.

Percentile

The value below which a specified percentage falls. One method of analysing frequency distributions is to present a given measure (for example income) above or below which a certain number of units (for example households, individuals, adults) fall. Thus the 90th percentile is the measure above which only 10 per cent of the units fall. **Quartiles** are the values of the given measure that divides the population into four equal-sized groups. The lowest quartile is the same as the 25th percentile. **Quintile**s are the values of the given measure that divides the population into five equal-sized groups. The lowest quintile is the same as the 20th percentile.

Personal pension scheme

A pension that is provided through a contract between an individual and the pension provider. The pension produced will be based on the level of contributions, investment returns and annuity rates. A personal pension can be either employer provided (for example a group personal pension) or purchased individually.

Private pension

See **Non-state pension**

Quartile

See **Percentile**

Quintile

See **Percentile**

Recently retired

Where the pensioner is less than five years over state pension age (60 for women and 65 for men).

Second tier pension provision

All contracted out personal and occupational pensions, and state second pension (S2P formerly SERPS), which includes all not contracted out pension scheme members. It is one of three tiers that have been defined to compare pensions systems on an international basis. The first tier is basic state retirement pension and means tested social benefits and the third tier covers additional voluntary contributions and personal pensions held in addition to second tier provision.

Self-administered pension scheme

A pension scheme in which the assets are invested by the trustees or an internal or external investment manager, rather than through an insurance contract with an insurance company.

Stakeholder pension

A personal pension product that complies with regulations that limit charges and allow individuals flexibility about contributions. Employers who do not provide an occupational scheme and are not otherwise exempt must offer their employees access to a stakeholder scheme.

State earnings-related pension scheme (SERPS)

The earnings-related additional pension provisions of the state pension scheme. It was replaced by the state second pension (S2P) from 6 April 2002.

State pension age (SPA)

The age from which pensions are normally payable by the state pension scheme. Currently age 60 for women and 65 for men, equalisation of SPA for both men and women at age 65 will be phased in between 2010 and 2020.

State second pension (S2P)

The additional pension provisions of the state pension scheme, linked to earnings and National Insurance contributions or credits built up during the working life. Replaced the state earnings-related pension scheme (SERPS) from 6 April 2002.

Status of pension scheme

An occupational pension scheme may be: **open** – scheme admits new members; **closed** – scheme does not admit new members but may continue to receive contributions from or on behalf of existing members who continue to accrue pension rights; **frozen** – a scheme under which benefits continue to be payable to existing members but to which no new members are admitted, no further contributions are payable and no further benefits accrue to existing members; **winding up**

– a scheme in the process of termination, either by buying annuities for the beneficiaries or by transferring assets and liabilities to another scheme.

Superannuation

Another term used for pension, particularly before the 1990s.

Transfer

A payment made from one pension scheme to another in lieu of benefits that have accrued to a transferring member, to enable the receiving scheme to provide alternative benefits.

Unfunded scheme

A scheme in which no fund is built up to provide in advance for pensions and other benefits. Such schemes may nevertheless charge employer and employee contributions, which help finance ongoing pension payments. Sometimes these contributions are set on the basis of a notional fund.

Working-age population

Generally defined as those aged 16–59 for women and 16–64 for men. However some analyses use a starting age of 20.